Marina Silva

Women Changing the World

Advisory Board for Women Changing the World

Marina Silva

Defending Rainforest Communities in Brazil

Ziporah Hildebrandt

The Feminist Press
at the City University of New York

Published by the Feminist Press at the City University of New York
The Graduate Center, 365 Fifth Avenue, New York, N.Y., 10016
feministpress.org

First edition, 2001

Library of Congress Cataloging-in-Publication Data

Hildebrandt, Ziporah.
    Marina Silva : defending rainforest communities in Brazil / Ziporah Hildebrandt
      p. cm. — (Women changing the world)
    Includes bibliographical references and index (p.).
    ISBN 1-55861-262-9 (Hardcover : alk. paper). — ISBN 1-55861-263-7 (pbk. : alk. paper.)
    1. Silva, Marina, 1958–   2. Women conservationists—Brazil—Biography.   3. Rainforest conservation—Brazil. I. Title. II. Series.

SD411.52.S55 H56 2001
333.75'16'092—dc21
[B]
                                        00-069165

The Feminist Press is grateful to Mariam K. Chamberlain, Florence Howe, Joanne Markell, and Genevieve Vaughan for their generosity in supporting this publication.

Design by Dayna Navaro
Composition by CompuDesign, Charlottesville, Virginia
Printed on acid-free paper by Transcontinental Printing
Printed in Canada

06   05   04   03   02   01   5   4   3   2   1

CONTENTS

WHAT DOES IT TAKE TO CHANGE THE WORLD?

Maybe this question sounds overwhelming. However, people who become leaders have all had to ask themselves this question at some point. They started finding answers by choosing how they would lead their lives every day and by creating their own opportunities to make a difference in the world. The anthropologist Margaret Mead said, "Never doubt that a small group of thoughtful, committed citizens can change the world; indeed it's the only thing that ever has." So let's look at some of the qualities possessed by people who are determined to change the world.

First, it takes vision. The great stateswoman and humanitarian Eleanor Roosevelt said, "You must do the thing you think you cannot do." People who change the world have the ability to see what is wrong in their society. They also have the ability to imagine something new and better. They do not accept the way things *are*—the "status quo"— as the only way things *must be* or *can be*. It is this vision of an improved world that inspires others to join leaders in their efforts to make change. Leaders are not afraid to be different, and the fear of failure does not prevent them from trying to create a better world.

Second, it takes courage. Mary Frances Berry, former head of the U.S. Commission on Civil Rights, said, "The time when you need to do something is when no one else is willing to do it, when people are saying it can't be done." People who change the world know that courage means more than just saying what needs to be changed. It means deciding to be active in the effort to bring about change—no matter what it takes. They know they face numerous challenges: they may be criticized, made fun of, ignored, alienated from their friends and family, imprisoned, or even killed. But even though they may sometimes feel scared, they continue to pursue their vision of a better world.

Third, it takes dedication and patience. The Nobel Prize–winning scientist Marie Curie said, "One never notices what has been done; one can only see what remains to be done." People who change the world understand that change does not happen overnight. Changing the world is an ongoing process. They also know that while what they do is important, change depends on what others do as well. Their original vision may transform and evolve over time as it interacts with the visions of others and as circumstances change. And they know that the job is never finished. Each success brings a new challenge, and each failure yet another obstacle to overcome.

Finally, it takes inspiration. People who change the world find strength in the experiences and accomplishments of others who came before them. Sometimes these role models are family members or personal friends. Sometimes they are great women and men who have spoken out and written about their own struggles to change the world for the better. Reading books about these people—learning about their lives and reading their own words—can be a source of inspiration for future world-changers. For example, when I was young, someone gave me a book called *Girls' Stories of Great Women,* which provided me with ideas of what women had achieved in ways I had never dreamed of and in places that were very distant from my small town. It helped me to imagine what I could do with my life and to know that I myself could begin working toward my goals.

This book is part of a series that introduces us to women who have changed the world through their vision, courage, determination, and patience. Their stories reveal their struggles as world-changers against obstacles such as poverty, discrimination, violence, and injustice. Their stories also tell of their struggles as women to overcome the belief, which still exists in most societies, that girls are less capable than boys of achieving high goals, and that women are less likely than men to become leaders. These world-changing women often needed even more vision and courage than their male counterparts, because as women they faced greater discrimination and resistance. They certainly needed more determination and patience, because no matter how much they proved themselves, there were always people who were reluctant to take their leadership and their achievements seriously, simply because they were women.

These women and many others like them did not allow these challenges to stop them. As they fought on, they found inspiration in women as well as men—their own mothers and grandmothers, and the great women who had come before them. And now they themselves stand as an inspiration to young women and men all over the world.

The women whose lives are described in this series come from different countries around the world and represent a variety of cultures. Their stories offer insights into the lives of people in varying circumstances. In some ways, their lives may seem very different from the lives of most people in the United States. We can learn from these differences as well as from the things we have in common. Women often share similar problems and concerns about issues such as violence in their lives and in the world, or the kind of environment we are creating for the future. Further, the qualities that enable women to become leaders, and to make positive changes, are often the same worldwide.

The books in this series tell the stories of women who have fought for justice and worked for positive change within their own societies. Some, like Marina Silva and Winona LaDuke, have struggled to protect the environment. In doing so, they are also struggling to protect the health and way of life of their people—the indigenous people who have lived on their land for many centuries.

One goal all of these women leaders share is to promote human rights—the basic rights to which all human beings are entitled. In 1948, the United Nations adopted the *Universal Declaration of Human Rights,* which outlines the rights of all people to freedom from slavery and torture, and to freedom of movement, speech, religion, and assembly, as well as rights of all people to social security, work, health, housing, education, culture, and citizenship. Further, it states that all people have the equal right to all these human rights, "without distinction of any kind such as race, color, sex, language . . . or other status."

In the United States, many of these ideas are not new to us. Some of them can be found in the first ten amendments to the U.S. Constitution, known as the Bill of Rights. Yet these ideals face continual challenges, and they must be defended and expanded by every generation. They have been tested in this country, for example, by the Civil Rights movement to end racial discrimination and the movement to bring about equal rights for women. They continue to be tested even today by various individuals and groups who are fighting for greater equality and justice.

All over the world, women and men work for and defend the common goal of human rights for all. In some places these rights are severely violated. Tradition and prejudice as well as social, economic, and political interests often exclude women, in particular, from benefitting from these basic rights. Over the past decade, women around the world have been questioning why women's rights and women's lives have been deemed secondary to human rights and the lives of men. As a result, an international women's human rights movement has emerged, with support from organizations such as the Center for Women's Global Leadership, to challenge limited ideas about human rights and to alert all nations that "women's rights are human rights."

The following biography is the true story of a woman overcoming incredible obstacles in order to peacefully achieve greater respect for human rights in her country. I am sure that you will find her story inspiring. I hope it also encourages you to join in the struggle to demand an end to all human rights violations—regardless of sex, race, class, or culture—throughout the world. And perhaps it will motivate you to become someone who just might change the world.

Charlotte Bunch
Founder and Executive Director
Center for Women's Global Leadership
Rutgers University

You can help to change the world now by establishing goals for yourself personally and by setting an example in how you live and work within your own family and community. You can speak out against unfairness and prejudice whenever you see it or hear it expressed by those around you. You can join an organization that is fighting for something you believe in, volunteer locally, or even start your own group in your school or neighborhood so that other people who share your beliefs can join you. Don't let anything or anyone limit your vision. Make your voice heard with confidence, strength, and dedication—and start changing the world today.

The people who live there know that the forest is a mystery. Everyone who lives in the Amazon thinks that the forest is something fabulous, a box of miraculous secrets that could explode at any moment.

—Marina Silva

Marina Silva, Brazilian senator from the state of Acre, in Amazonia

Chapter 1

GIRL FROM THE RAINFOREST

A thin young woman with dark, flashing eyes stood—fierce and determined—with a dozen others. Their strong, brown arms linked them together as their voices rang out in an inspiring song. But the roar of bulldozers and chain saws blasted their harmonies.

A work crew had been ordered to clear the rainforest. Giant trees, plants, and animals would die to make a cattle pasture. The families living on the land would lose everything: homes, gardens, the rubber trees that sustained their meager living—their whole way of life.

The young woman, Marina Silva, tightened her arms with the men beside her as a worker came close. Marina looked him in the eyes as he made his chain saw whine angrily. He brought it within inches of their linked arms.

Marina didn't flinch, though she and the others were all that stood between the saws and the rainforest. She and her neighbors lived by harvesting, or tapping, rubber from the trees. Although they were poor and had little power in Brazil's unjust society, the rubber tappers had found a way to fight for their forest life. One demonstration at a time, they worked to save their rubber trees from rich cattle ranchers.

Don't cut these trees, Marina prayed silently.

The voice of her group's leader, Chico Mendes, rang out. "Why help the rich boss take away our homes?" he said to the workers. "We should stand together, help each other—that's the way we both can live."

The worker was young, in his twenties—Marina's age. His eyes met hers doubtfully, then slid away. "I need the money," he mumbled.

"Of course," Marina answered. "We all do. But is it right that you make a little cash by taking away our rubber trees? You'll have money in your pocket for a few days, a few weeks, and then what? When the trees are cut, the boss will fire you. You'll be hungry again, and so will we because we won't have anything. It's the boss who gets rich from our work and our land."

The worker nodded in agreement. A shot rang out, but Marina kept her gaze locked on the young man. "The boss thinks nothing of killing us," Chico Mendes shouted. "You and your family could be next. We have to stand together."

Destruction of vast areas of rainforest often begin with cutting trees for sale as valuable lumber. Later the land is cleared for cattle ranching and farming.

But more shots were fired, and someone cried out. At the other end of the line, the work crew was beating the unarmed demonstrators with clubs. The young man Marina was talking to put down his saw and disappeared into the forest. Then Marina covered her head as the clubs crashed down.

The *seringueiros* (SAY-reeng-GAY-rowz), or rubber tappers, did not strike back. They retreated into the forest, carrying hurt friends. One young man had been shot and would probably die. Marina heard his mother and sister crying.

This demonstration had failed, but the *seringueiros* would try again and again. They knew that by fighting for the rainforest, they were fighting for their lives.

Marina had grown up in the *seringal,* the rubber-tapping region of Amazonia. The rainforest was her people's life. They loved their trees as friends and relatives. Marina dreamed that her people would be recognized for their character and their knowledge of the forest, rather than scorned for their poverty and illiteracy. She dreamed of a day when all forest people would be safe in their homes, and earn a decent living from their traditional ways. Forest people and communities would control their own lives instead of suffering under the brutal power of wealthy ranchers, business people, and politicians.

Most people shook their heads at Marina's dreams. Things had always been this way. How could they change? But that didn't stop her. "First the dream, then the fight," she later said. Already her impossible dreams had brought her from illiterate poverty to the doors of a top university—in Brazil, a journey more spectacular than Cinderella's dance from rags

Rainforests are the most biologically diverse environments on the earth, as well as some of the most beautiful. The dense forest is mixed with streams and waterfalls, tributaries of the Amazon River.

This macaque is one of hundreds of species of monkeys found in tropical rainforests throughout the world. Macaques need the tall, leafy trees for to live in, to hide from predators, and to find food such as fruit, nuts, and insects.

to riches. No magic was involved: Marina had come every step of the way on determination, intelligence, and dreams.

If her dream of getting an education could come true, why not her dream for forest people? She didn't know then that her dream would bring her to the highest chambers of Brazil's government. As senator for her state of Acre (AH-kray) she was one of only five women in the senate. Born in poverty, she spoke out for women and the poor all over Brazil. In years to come, Marina, who couldn't read until she was sixteen years old, would fly to the world's most powerful countries and discuss the fate of the rainforest and its peoples with presidents, prime ministers, and the pope. The *seringueiros'* peaceful demonstrations would lead to a totally new way to save millions of acres of forest.

Today, in a country that has always been run by the rich, Marina speaks out and uses her power for the poor. In a world where easy money triumphs daily over human need, Marina speaks for the future and against human suffering. In a society where politicians often get votes with lies and bribes, then use their office to make money, Marina is honest and unselfish.

Her state of Acre is in Amazonia, the largest remaining rainforest on earth. When Brazil's government decided to build in Amazonia, settlers and cattle ranchers burned thousands of miles of forest to make farms and pasture. But the soil was thin and poor. Crops failed. Farmers gave up and moved west to freshly cleared land.

They left behind a desert. The rainforest acts like a sponge: It soaks up rain, uses it to grow, and releases moisture back into the atmosphere to make

Tributaries of the Amazon River reach across South America just below the equator, through Brazil and into Colombia, Ecuador, Peru, and Bolivia. The water and wildlife of the river affect the lives of millions of people along the way.

more rain. Dense layers of leaves protect the thin soil. Without trees, the soil washed away, then baked hard in the tropical heat.

Brazil's government didn't know how people could make a living from this land. Yet people have lived for tens of thousands of years in the forest. By growing food, fishing, and gathering the natural products of the forest, indigenous peoples and *seringueiros* have lived well and brought valuable goods to market. They understand what the government does not: how to take from the forest without destroying it.

Senator Marina Silva hopes to teach Brazil and the rich countries of the world how to do the same. Otherwise the rainforest and its peoples will vanish from the earth forever.

Chapter 2

LESSONS FROM THE TREES

Maria Osmarina Marina da Silva Vaz de Lima, called Marina Silva, is one of eleven children born to Maria Augusta and Pedro Augusto da Silva. Marina is the second oldest of their eight surviving children. She was born in the rainy season, on February 8, 1958, in Breu Velho, in Seringal Bagaço (sair-een-GALL ba-GAH-soo). A *seringal* is an area of rainforest where rubber trees are tapped. The names of *seringals* and the clearings where people live are rainforest addresses. Seringal Bagaço is seventy kilometers—about forty miles—east of Rio Branco, the capital of the state of Acre, in the far west of Brazil's Amazon region.

"We feel sorry for Pedro; having daughters is a major setback," his neighbors said when nine of their babies were girls. Girls and women in the *seringal* usually worked around the house and garden. They took care of children, gardens, and animals, and gathered fruit, nuts, and plants from the forest. Families looked to men and boys to do the hardest physical work. Boys started at nine or ten years old helping their fathers tap rubber trees, hunt, fish, and clear patches of forest for gardens. Every family wanted boys to help with these jobs that made money.

When Marina's mother gave birth, she had no hospital and no doctor. Rio Branco was less than forty-five miles away, but there were no roads through the rainforest or cars to get there. The only way to travel far in Amazonia was on winding, twisting rivers.

Medical treatment meant several days in a small boat. Midwives delivered babies in the forest, and their knowledge and long experience handled most problems. But when trouble required medical supplies and equipment, nothing could be done to save lives.

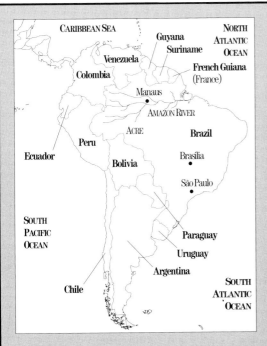

What is Brazil like?

Brazil is the largest country in South America and the fifth largest in the world. It has the world's third largest city—São Paulo—and sells the most citrus fruit and coffee. Brazil also has the world's biggest river and rainforest. Most of the country has a tropical climate.

The area that today makes up Brazil was colonized by Portugal in 1500. Portuguese is still the national language, and the majority of people are Catholic. Brazil's coastal forests were cleared for cattle ranching and growing sugarcane. Indigenous people and at least 3.65 million people brought from Africa were enslaved on plantations, outnumbering the white colonists.

Later, poor farmers from Europe flocked to Brazil's south to grow coffee. Today the south is Brazil's high tech region, and family farmers are turned off the land by big businesses.

Religious missionaries and explorers settled along Amazonia's rivers and ventured into the dangerous rainforest, eager to convert indigenous people to Christianity or to take gold, slaves, and other wealth. African slaves escaped to the deep forest and built hidden towns there.

Many different peoples—indigenous, African, European—have contributed to Brazil's distinctive culture. Brazilians are proud of their mixed heritage and their famous artists, musicians, athletes, scientists, and thinkers.

Marina's first brother died when he was one week old from an infection in his umbilical cord, which wasn't well sterilized when it was cut. For many years the family had no son, so Pedro looked to his oldest daughters for the help he needed to support the family.

Still, eight surviving children was more than Marina's parents expected. Many families had only three or four living children. Everyone wanted a big family. Children were a blessing.

Most people in Brazil are a mix of indigenous, African, and European peoples. Marina's parents are of Afro-Brazilian heritage, descended from European colonists and enslaved Africans brought to Brazil centuries ago. Like most *seringueiros,* they are *nordestino,* from Brazil's northeast, and proud of their roots. This dry, crowded, infertile area is one of the poorest in the western hemisphere. One of the first places in the Americas to be colonized by Europeans, the northeastern forests were quickly cleared to plant sugarcane. Slaves worked the sugarcane fields. Cattle grazed on grass and scrub, and gave beef to feed the rich planters and the slaves.

Cattle and sugarcane are still the northeast's main crops. The land is divided into enormous cattle ranches, some as big as small countries in Europe. Poor farmers struggle to grow food on land that belongs to the rich ranch owners. Every few years a drought turns life from difficult to impossible. Millions flee the northeast, looking for food, work, or land elsewhere. Some have become rubber tappers in Brazil's rainforests.

Because heavy rain may make thick mud or streams overflow, houses in many rubber tappers' clearings are built on stilts off the ground. Houses are made from what is found in the forest—palm logs and branches.

Until she was old and strong enough to do adult work at age nine, Marina, like most children in the *seringal,* had other jobs. She swept the house and hauled water for cooking, washing, and drinking. She helped with laundry, watched the babies, weeded the garden, and gathered fruit and firewood.

Her home was a typical Amazonian house built of palm logs and roofed with palm leaves—the same way *seringueiros* build houses today. The house stood on stilts. It rained every day and the ground was often puddled and slippery. A shaded porch along one open side kept the house cool. The cookstove was on a platform sticking out from the rest of the house, so the heat went out, not in. The floors had spaces between the logs so water drained out and food scraps dropped through for the chickens and ducks, which also ate mosquitoes and bugs living in the shade under the house.

Food was often scarce. Collecting rubber and Brazil nuts didn't pay enough to buy food for a family to eat well. Hunting, fishing, and gardening were necessary, but even this was not always enough. Most families ate only one real meal each day, around noon. What a *seringueiro* ate in a whole day would be considered only enough for one meal by most people in North America or Europe.

Sometimes the rubber boss forbade gardens, and *seringueiros* lived near starvation. Other families didn't have gardens because the children were too small to help and the fathers were too busy with rubber tapping to cut and clear trees to make space to plant food. Clearing land is heavy, difficult work;

One natural product of rainforests is the latex sap of rubber trees—a sticky liquid which is turned into solid rubber. Harvesting the sap doesn't hurt the tree, if done right. So tappers can earn money time after time for a lifetime, without destroying the forest or forest animals' habitat.

Who are Brazil's indigenous people?

Indigenous people are the original human inhabitants of a region. In Brazil, these are the many nations who have lived there for over thirty thousand years. Until recently people thought that indigenous nations in the Americas were few and widely scattered—only a million people in Amazonia. Recent estimates put Amazonia's population before the arrival of Columbus closer to 20 million.

Today the same number of people live in the Amazon, but just a small fraction of them are indigenous people. First contacts with Europeans brought epidemics—diseases which indigenous people had never seen and couldn't resist or treat—which may have killed 90 percent of the native population. Also indigenous people were subject to intense racial prejudice and were usually enslaved. When they fought back they were killed or scattered. Now there are only around 250,000 indigenous people in all of Brazil. They form 215 ethnic groups that speak about 170 languages.

Modern ideas about indigenous peoples are changing. More people recognize that cultural diversity is precious, and that indigenous people have the right to protect their way of life.

rainforest trees are immense, and few people owned tools bigger than a machete.

Children often had weak health from poor nutrition. They usually had parasites in their digestive tracts, which could make them very sick. Drugs used to get rid of parasites were not always effective. They could also be toxic, or poisonous if misused. Malaria, transmitted by mosquitoes, was the worst problem. People can get sick from it again and again, and without treatment they often die. Marina has had malaria five times. Marina also contracted leishmaniasis from the bite of a sandfly. Leishmaniasis causes sores, especially on the face.

When they get sick, many Brazilians will take pills, use medicinal plants, pray to saints, and visit a healer, hoping that any one of these may cure the illness. They may visit a *pajé* (PAH-zhay), or a practitioner of indigenous magic and healing. Most forest people believe illness can be caused by forest spirits. Over-hunting, eating certain kinds of animals at certain times, going to certain places in the forest, and many other actions offend the spirits. *Pajés* treat sickness with both medicinal plants and rituals or by performing a sacred action that connects the *pajé* to the spirit world.

About the forest Marina learned that each kind of creature has a "Mother of the Animal" that protects it from overhunting by causing accidents or stealing a person's shadow, which makes the person sick. The "Mother of the Waters" tips over the canoe of people who catch more fish than they need. Most famous of all is Caboclinho da Mata, the "Little Man of the Forest," whose feet are turned backwards. He lures hunters and dogs deeper and deeper into the forest, until they are lost forever.

To Marina, these stories and beliefs taught the lesson of the forest: Take only what you need, so that others may live and life continue. The rubber tree teaches the same lesson: Cut only so deep, or the tree will die; don't cut every day, or the tree will grow tired. It is a lesson that the government of Brazil—and the world—is learning too slowly: The rainforest gives life only when it is healthy and whole. Once damaged, it means death. Until recently this powerful value system guided the forest people's lives and sustained their livelihood.

Marina's grandmother taught her the principles of the Catholic faith. Though most people in Brazil were Catholics, there were no churches in remote areas. Traveling priests performed weddings, funerals, and other rites. Their visits were often festive occasions

The Amazon flows for thousands of miles, and its tropical ecosystem is the greatest single source of biodiversity on the earth. The beautiful river has, in places, been polluted with mining chemicals and mercury. Long sections have turned bright yellow or brown and are dangerous to animals and people.

with food, dancing, and soccer. The priests brought statues of saints with them, such as St. Benedict, the protector of rubber trees. Marina heard tales of the statues curing illness and walking about at night.

But these tales were not enough for Marina's curious and questioning mind. She wrote, "One of my biggest problems during my childhood was to find out who God was and where He had come from." She pestered her grandmother with questions about why God did this, and why things are like that. "Even if I had never seen a bible and I had never entered church, I started a journey." It was her way of learning and making sense of the world. She built her own foundation of understanding and critical thinking.

Marina was very aware, even when young, of the precariousness of her family's existence. Forest people are expert ecologists. They learn from their daily lives that every living thing has a place in the network of the forest. Keeping the rubber and Brazil nut trees alive was a matter of life and death to Marina. She often worried about what would happen if the trees died. Her father would have no work. She and her family would have nothing to live on. She was afraid of the trees dying from mistreatment at the hands of temporary workers her father hired. They sometimes cut deeply into the tree and extracted such a quantity of latex sap it ruined or killed the tree.

There is a tree called *massaranduba* with sap, Marina said, which "looked like blood—the milk of the heart." It frightened her. It was as if the forest itself was bleeding. She tended its wound with clay, believing she gave it medicine.

Why is Amazonia unique?

Amazonia contains the largest river system in the world. Almost 4,000 miles long, practically a quarter of the earth's running fresh water is in the Amazon and its over 1,000 tributaries. The river's mouth, where it meets the Atlantic Ocean, is over two hundred miles wide, and it is so deep that ocean-going vessels can reach Peru.

Amazonia is vast, and much about it remains unknown. Over a third of all the species of plants and animals on the earth live here. More species of fish live in Amazonia than in the Atlantic Ocean. It is the largest rainforest left, and the largest tropical ecosystem on the earth, filled with mystery, beauty, and biological treasure. And it is being destroyed so fast that every day a species disappears—extinct without ever being known.

From time to time false rumors ran through the forest. "No one is buying Brazil nuts," and "No one can sell rubber." These rumors scared Marina.

She planted her own forest of rubber trees in a clearing as insurance in case something were to kill the forest. But rubber trees take years to grow big enough to tap. And like most other kinds of rainforest trees, diseases and pests attack rubber trees that are growing too close together. Her family moved to another part of the *seringal* long before her trees could be tapped.

Like most Brazilians, Marina's father was eager for a better life. When Marina was seven, her father moved the family to Manaus (man-OUSE), Amazonia's only big city. From Acre they traveled down the winding Purus River about 1400 kilometers—almost 900 miles—on a boat. In Manaus, Pedro set up a small store and bar. But the business went bankrupt in five months.

On the advice of Pedro's brother, they continued another 1200 kilometers downriver to Santa Maria, a town near the mouth of the Amazon. Prices for manioc—a large, nutritious root vegetable—were high there, and Pedro set to work planting. Brazilians eat *farinha*, roasted manioc flour, with almost every meal, and manioc is made into many tasty dishes.

But manioc prices fell, and so did the family's earnings. For the first time the family knew real hunger. On the *seringal* they had rainforest fruits, nuts, animals, and fish. They could buy on credit from the rubber boss's store. In Santa Maria there was no rainforest and no credit.

"At first," Marina remembers, "we gave up the meat, eating just rice and beans. But later there were times we wouldn't eat at all for twenty-four hours. I recall an Easter Saturday when my mother served flour with only one egg." Her parents didn't eat at all that day.

After nearly two years of suffering, Pedro's old boss at Seringal Bagaço agreed to pay for their trip back. But the family would have to produce extra rubber to repay him. Rubber prices were very low. Pedro's work wasn't enough to pay off the large debt along with food, medicine, and other supplies. For a long time to come, the family would be back where they started—in debt to the rubber boss.

During the four-week journey back up the Amazon, Marina and her sisters watched river dolphins play alongside the boat. Huge fish, snakes, otters, jaguars, and many other animals swam the river. Parrots and other birds cried from the shore. Butterflies, flowers, and fruit brightened the green forest. It was the last free time they would have for years.

Many Amazon trees grow extra roots for support in the poor, shallow soil. Most of the plants in Amazonia have not been studied. Many have never been named. Any of these might have valuable uses, such as new treatments for disease.

A year later, twelve-year-old Marina awoke on a typical day. She stepped out of her family's house. The sky was still the black of the long tropical night. Her long, black braid hung to the waist of a worn-out dress that was almost too small. She fastened a kerosene lamp to her head and she carried a sack, a shotgun, and an angled knife. In the dark before dawn, she headed toward the forest, stopping to light her lamp with a match.

Along the narrow trail was a big rubber tree with rows of scars along its trunk. With her knife Marina carefully cut into the bark, a certain distance from the last cut. White latex sap oozed from the long cut. She propped a cup made from a tin can to catch the milky sap, and continued along the trail. She went quickly, for she had miles to go before returning home for the main meal of the day. Marina was now a full-time *seringueira*.

Most *seringueiros* know the story of rubber. Thousands of years ago, indigenous people discovered that latex sap from rubber trees made containers

A rainforest home's kitchen is often outside the house, at least in part. Including gathering vegetables and fruit from gardens and the forest, feeding a family can require the work of many people. Children often share the important job with their parents.

waterproof. They played with bouncy balls they made from the rubber. By the early 1800s, hundreds of thousands of waterproof boots, knapsacks, and rubber erasers were made in Brazil for sale in Europe and North America. In 1839, English chemist Charles Goodyear discovered a treatment that made rubber useful for hoses, tires, and many other things.

Rubber trees grew only in Amazonia. Like a gold rush, thousands of people headed to the rainforest looking for rubber. Rich businessmen took the indigenous nations' land. At least seventy nations— hundreds of thousands of people—were destroyed: enslaved, murdered, or killed by European diseases.

The new owners of vast stretches of rainforest, now called rubber estates, forced people to tap trees for them. Many *seringueiros* died of malaria or other diseases, but the survivors started families, often with kidnapped indigenous wives. *Seringueiros,* taught in large part by their indigenous wives, learned how to live in the forest.

The landowners grew enormously rich and lived in luxury. They built fancy public buildings and wore expensive clothes. They sent their laundry to Europe to be cleaned and their children there to school. They were so rich that Manaus was one of the first cities in the world to be wired for electricity.

Then an Englishman smuggled 70,000 seeds from rubber trees out of Brazil. These seeds grew huge plantations in Asia. Suddenly Brazil wasn't the only source of rubber. The price of rubber fell, and the wealth dried up.

Later, the invention of the automobile required rubber for tires, and the demand for rubber grew. During World War II Japan controlled the Asian

Huge rubber trees grow from these tiny seeds. Thousands of seeds like these were secretly smuggled out of Brazil in the 1800s to start plantations elsewhere, taking away a big piece of the rubber fortune.

plantations, so the United States turned back to Amazonia for rubber. Poor *nordestinos* from Brazil's drought-stricken northeast were lured to Acre's rubber estates. Thousands boarded boats and headed up the Amazon River, singing patriotic songs about rubber saving the free world. Almost half died of malaria or cruel treatment from the rubber bosses. When the war was over rubber prices dropped again as demand went down. Soon, with the invention of synthetic rubber, the price dropped even more.

Extracting rubber, Brazil nuts, and other products from the forest was the only livelihood most Amazonians had. Debt to landowners and falling prices locked them into poverty.

As she walked through the forest that morning, a rustle beside young Marina alerted her. She turned her head and her lamp shone on hundreds of ants carrying their babies to higher ground before the heavy rains. Marina loved the intricate, ever-changing web of forest life. She smiled and went on her way, careful where she stepped.

Rubber tappers cut hundreds of trees each day, without hurting the tree, to collect the precious sap that runs out. Rubber trees are spread out over miles of jungle, and tappers must walk far carrying the heavy sap. You can see the many cuts on the tree trunk, each one marking a day's work for the tapper.

A jaguar climbs through the trees in the rainforest. Jaguars can be over four feet long and weigh two hundred pounds. They cover miles and miles of forest every day, and need a big territory to find enough food. Because of lost habitat, one fifth of the world's species are at risk of extinction in the next thirty years.

At the next rubber tree, she made another cut, not too deep. She positioned a cup—this one made from the outer husk of the Brazil nut pod—and hurried to the next tree, and the next. It was important to hurry, for the sap flows most freely in the morning.

Full daylight soon filtered through the forest canopy over one hundred feet above. Marina doused the lamp's flame, though the light was still dim on the forest floor. A band of howler monkeys leapt through the canopy. She peered upward toward their deafening calls and held the gun ready. Killing a monkey made her heart ache, but her mother, father, sisters, and brother needed to eat, and meat was scarce. But she saw only shaking branches through the dense leaves.

By the time the trail ended back at the house, Marina had walked ten miles and tapped almost one hundred rubber trees.

Marina called a greeting to her older sister in the garden. Her name is Maria Delzimar, but Marina and her sisters called her De Deusa, "of goddess" in Portuguese. Most people in Brazil have a nickname. Brazilians like unusual or famous names along with family names. But Marina's mother always called the girls by their given names.

Marina's mother made a meal of rice, beans, vegetables, and peppers sprinkled with *farinha*, all from their garden. The whole family ate and talked. Marina's father also spent the morning tapping rubber trees. When he finished eating and stood up, Marina did, too. She got a sack to collect the latex, and went to the same trail she set out on that morning. Sometimes her mother and De Deusa collected the sap, but not today. They were needed at the house because one of Marina's younger sisters was sick.

Fresh latex makes the best rubber. Marina collected the morning's sap, emptying each cup into her sack. It was hard work, too hard for most girls, but Marina was much stronger than her mother and sisters. Some trees were cut so many times she had to climb a notched pole leaning against the tree to reach the cup. Her sack got heavier. Soon she had to walk the long way home to empty it, then return to get the rest of the latex.

Marina was always alert to the forest around her. The calls and movements of birds, monkeys, frogs, and insects told Marina about and what was happening in the forest, when it would rain, which fruits or nuts were ripe. Jaguars and poisonous snakes were shy, but there were other dangers: deadly spiders, thorny bushes, ants with burning bites, warnings from forest spirits. There was also the chance of shooting a big jungle bird, armadillo, or perhaps a delicious paca, a striped rodent the size of a rabbit.

Parrots, along with toucans, hummingbirds, and countless other birds live among the shady trees and bright sun of Amazonia. Many North American songbirds spend the winter in South and Central American forests. They need the diversity of fruit and flowers of the rainforest to live.

The sticky latex sap that runs in rubber trees can be heated and turned into a solid block of rubber, which then can be stored until it is needed to make tires, mattresses, sports equipment, and other products.

Finally the miles were walked, and the cups were emptied, making several gallons of sap for the day. But before she could eat and rest, the latex had to be cured in the smoking hut. It was slow, hot, dirty work.

Marina and her father, Pedro, poured the sap little by little onto a strong stick, all the while turning it over a smoky fire. Indigenous people have treated latex this way for thousands of years. The smoke hardens and preserves the latex, making a high-quality rubber that fetches a good price. Oily palm nuts burned in the fire made thick, foul-smelling smoke that got in Marina's eyes, hair, and clothes and made her cough. When their ball of rubber was big enough, usually over ninety pounds, her father took it off the stick and stacked it with the rubber going by mule to the boss's store.

Marina and her father talked while they worked. She was full of questions, and loved to hear his stories. Sometimes he taught her addition, subtraction, and multiplication. No one in the family had been to school, but unlike many *seringueiros,* Pedro knew enough arithmetic to keep the rubber boss from cheating him.

At last, Marina could wash and go into the house to help her mother feed the littlest children. She ate some fruit and a handful of *farinha,* then went to bed. It felt good to rest in her hammock after the long day's work. Marina kept a copy of the alphabet someone wrote down for her, and she peered at it, working to memorize the letters. Then the lamp was put out. In the utter darkness, she felt the hopelessness of ever changing this life, then the night symphony of rainforest creatures' noises put her to sleep.

Chapter 3
OUT OF DEBT SLAVERY

Marina had two impossible dreams: to be a nun and to go to school. Most *seringueiros* couldn't do arithmetic, read, or even write their own names. The landowners did not provide schools in the rubber estates. Without schooling, Marina could not become a nun. It seemed she was too poor to be anything but what she was.

There was little money on the *seringal*. Every time the family took rubber to the store, the boss weighed it. He subtracted the value of the rubber from the amount they owed him. The debt shrank. Then they bought supplies on credit, increasing the debt again. They made many useful things from forest materials, but some things had to come from the store, like medicine, cooking pots, tools, clothing, matches, and kerosene for lamps. Since this was the only store in the *seringal,* the boss could charge whatever he wanted.

The *seringueiros* were isolated from the rest of Brazil. With no electricity, telephones, libraries, or newspapers, they didn't know what things really cost. The rubber bosses sold supplies at high, unfair prices. This system, in which people become slaves to debt, is known as *aviamento. Aviamento* benefitted the rubber bosses by keeping the *seringueiros* ignorant and poor. They worked their whole lives for the boss and died still in debt. Loyalty was very important; the boss got angry if one of "his" tappers sold rubber elsewhere. Disloyal tappers were beaten or

People who work for rubber plantations are often forced to borrow money from their boss just to survive. Once in debt the workers are treated as slaves, and, like these men, are shipped wherever the boss needs workers. They can be kicked out of their homes at any time if the boss decides to sell the land.

killed to frighten other *seringueiros*. When tappers tried to escape, they were hunted down and severely punished.

Aviamento came from Brazil's colonial days, when the plantation owner held the power of life and death over his family and slaves. The attitudes this created in both rich and poor people are deeply ingrained in Brazilian society. The wealthy look down on physical labor, and consider it their right to take what they want and order people around. Workers like *seringueiros*, with little money or education, have few choices about their own lives, and often don't believe that they could succeed even if they tried.

The name of Marina's home, Seringal Bagaço, reflects the realities of life there. *Bagaço* is the useless pulp left after the sweet juice of the sugarcane is squeezed out.

One day in 1970, Marina's father patted their stack of rubber and smiled at her. His daughters had worked very hard in the past year. So hard, the

Processed rubber is sold and shipped to cities or other countries to be made into products. This worker, who belongs to a rubber cooperative, will share the profits from the rubber equally with the families who tapped and heated it, rather than all the money going to one plantation boss. Organizing workers into unions helped bring about this new way of doing business.

family had done that rare thing: repaid their debt.

Now the family could try to save some money for the future, perhaps for an opportunity to improve their lives. They continued to work hard.

By the time Marina was fourteen, she knew everything anyone could teach her about the rainforest but very little about the world beyond the forest. She had never been around television, electric lights, or flush toilets. Her family had enough to eat, but the future was still so uncertain.

Brazil was changing. In 1964, when Marina was six, the democratically elected president of Brazil was forced from office. Brazil's military took over, with the support of the United States. The military leaders chose a general to be president. In the next few years, the regime ruled by terror, and murdered, exiled, or imprisoned anyone they didn't trust.

While many Brazilians lived in fear of arrest and torture, the *seringueiros'* lives stayed much the same. Everyone was poor. Rubber prices were extremely low

What is a military regime?

When a nation is run by its army, that government is called a military regime. Brazil's generals seized control of the country in 1964. Then they began getting rid of their opponents. Over the next five years, about 50,000 people were arrested, and thousands died. The regime used violence, terror, and harsh laws to control the country and stay in power.

The regime needed the support of the United States, the World Bank, and other powerful bodies, so Brazil needed to appear democratic. The regime permitted controlled national and local elections, but only approved candidates were allowed. All political parties except its own were outlawed. People at meetings or protests risked arrest, injury, or death. Fear or unfair voting laws kept most poor people from voting. The regime decided what was printed in newspapers or broadcast on television or radio. Without accurate information about events people had difficulty uniting to create change.

The regime also controlled the courts. Judges appointed by the regime were told what to decide. Anyone with friends in the government could commit serious crimes knowing they would not be punished. Ordinary people were arrested and imprisoned without committing a crime. Although many countries have constitutions that protect their people from such abuses of power, the regime changed Brazil's constitution and made new laws.

because Brazil's economy was in terrible shape. But politics didn't influence forest people much. There were no workers' unions for them, and indigenous and illiterate people weren't allowed to vote.

Then change came to the *seringal*. The regime began to develop Amazonia. Brazil had major economic problems: soaring prices and worthless money, enormous debt to richer countries, and over a third of the population in desperate need of homes, food, jobs, land, schools, hospitals, roads, and basic services like clean water. The regime wanted to show the world it was working to solve Brazil's problems.

On a map, Amazonia looked blank to the generals.

They saw an area almost as large as Europe, but with no roads at all, and just a few small cities and towns. The regime thought Amazonia's empty space might be developed and turned into farms, factories, and iron and gold mines to make money, pay their debt, and make Brazil a world power. They didn't care about the indigenous people, *seringueiros,* and others living in the rainforest.

The regime was also afraid of the poor. The rich had always run Brazil. The regime wanted to keep land, wealth, and power in the hands of the old families they thought deserved it. They feared Brazil's poor would band together to take control of the land and their lives. Millions of poor farmers in the northeast and south were demanding farmland the rich owned but didn't use. Why not give them land in Amazonia instead?

In 1970, the government began building the high-ways into Amazonia. The government also started a huge project to move farmers and their families, called settlers, into Rôndonia (hon-DOE-nya), the state east of Acre. The governor of Acre wanted to develop Acre at the same time.

The first step was building roads. Once bulldozers pushed down trees, then came settlers, gold prospectors, business people, ranchers, and people buying and selling the land for quick profit. Thousands of miles of rainforest were burned along the new roads.

Indigenous nations that had never been contacted were sought out. Specialists tried to communicate with the indigenous people so they wouldn't fight back when their lands were invaded. Indigenous people would need modern medicines when they began to die of European diseases like smallpox.

After the military takeover of Brazil in 1964, tanks and the army patrolled city streets, frightening and intimidating people who might have wanted an elected government. The military was also known for violence against homeless people and people who spoke out against the regime.

Bulldozers cleared miles and miles of rainforest to make room for ranchers to graze their cattle, for roads to be built, and for settlers to start new farms. Sometimes the valuable trees were used for lumber. Often they were simply burned.

Sometimes the government set aside large areas of land as reserves for indigenous nations. Other people weren't allowed in these reserves without permission, but poachers, loggers, prospectors, drug smugglers, and settlers ignored the rules. These invaders brought more sickness, violence, and disruption to indigenous communities. They contaminated water with diseases and mining chemicals. They hunted animals and stole from or destroyed village gardens. The highway and colonization project were disasters for indigenous people.

New roads and people brought changes to the *seringal,* too. Because of low prices, many rubber estate owners were in debt. They sold their rainforest land to ranchers, who cleared and burned the forest. New laws had given the ranchers money—called subsidies—as encouragement to turn rainforest into pasture. And the new highway gave the ranchers just what they needed to ship cattle to market.

But Highway BR-364 into Acre was unpaved, often a sea of mud that trapped settlers' buses for days. Truckloads of produce rotted before they got to market. Still, Acre's governor dreamed of a time when money in Acre would not come from a few nut and rubber gatherers. IIis vision for Acre was green pastures and white cattle. He began to sell the land in Acre, even land the state didn't own. More of Acre was sold than actually existed.

BR-364 brought thousands of settlers to Acre looking for land. Millions of poor farming families had been forced from their land to make way for electric power plants, for mines, or for giant farms growing food for sale in Europe or North America, often as animal feed. The government had promised these poor farmers land in Amazonia, along with tools and seeds to help them start over. As many as 7,000 families a week crowded onto buses to go to Amazonia.

"It was like we had entered into a different reality," Marina remembers. The government settlement

Brazilian activist Chico Mendes stands on Highway BR-364 as it is being built. Twelve miles of forest was cleared on each side of the road. Chico Mendes and others opposed the thoughtless destruction of the forest.

How does development affect indigenous people?

When development comes too quickly, or without consulting the people who live in a place and who know it best, this can destroy not only the ecology, but cultural diversity as well.

Careless development hurts indigenous people more than anyone else. When their land is invaded and destroyed and nations can no longer feed themselves, government handouts can make groups forget their traditional ways of living. Once a group sees technology, it can never go back to the way it was. The strength of guns, bulldozers, airplanes, radios, and antibiotics can make traditions look weak. When a nation loses faith in its traditions, its people can lose the will to live, and illness, depression, addiction, and suicide can strike. In 1995, fifty Kaiowá-Guarani under the age of twenty committed suicide.

Cultural heritage and expert knowledge of land, plants, and animals amassed over thousands of years are lost, along with unique ways of viewing the world and solving human problems. We all learn from those who are different from us—some experts think this is essential to human survival. When a nation dies, its culture is lost to everyone.

agency drew lines on a map to divide the land along the road into plots of 247 acres. Though the plots looked equal on the map, they weren't. Some were under water. Some belonged to indigenous people. A few had good soil; most did not. Some were already the homes of *seringueiros,* Marina's family included.

When Marina was fifteen, Seringal Bagaço disappeared in a patchwork of settlement plots. Marina's family and the other *seringueiros* had no choice: they got a plot like the settlers—the land they lived on. The plots were much too small to include the hundreds of rubber trees they needed to tap each day. *Seringueiros* turned to farming. Some sold their plots and moved to the city in search of work.

The settlers cut the trees on their plots, let them

dry, then burned them. The ash enriched the soil for planting rice, coffee, cocoa, manioc, and other crops. But valuable timber like mahogany was burned along with rubber, Brazil nut, palm, and other useful trees. The orchids, vines, and other plants that provided homes in the forest canopy for frogs, snakes, insects, birds, and thousands of other small creatures all burned. Burnt animals limped along, looking for new homes. For weeks the air of Acre was filled with smoke.

The settlers had few tools; the promised government help had never arrived. Parents made holes with long sticks for children to drop seeds into. They hurried to get everything planted between the smoldering tree trunks. The rainy season would come soon.

New diseases came, too. Malaria mosquitoes thrive in standing water. Most rainforest water flows in rivers and streams. But the bulldozers left pools and puddles behind, breeding many more mosquitoes. In addition, the settlers brought new strains of malaria. Five epidemics hit, killing Marina's three-year-old sister, Deusilene. Then Maria Rosilene, six months old, died of measles and malaria. Marina had malaria five times, but she survived.

The next epidemic was meningitis, a serious infection that affects the brain and spinal cord. Marina was fourteen when, one afternoon, her mother felt sick. Now that there was a road, medical help was possible. A cousin went to get a taxi, worrying that it might be meningitis. The driver was afraid of getting infected, so Marina's cousin said it was just malaria or a fever.

Marina's mother's headache was terrible. When a taxi finally came, Marina's father and De Deusa took

Children, like this young boy, are often the most vulnerable to illness, especially in poor communities where no one gets enough to eat. Most poor rainforest families have at least one child die in their early years. Malnutrition is part of the problem, but epidemic diseases brought from outside Amazonia could strike anyone, adult or child.

their mother to the hospital. Marina and the younger children went to their grandmother's house.

Her mother had told Marina to clean and cook, as her grandmother wouldn't be able to care for six young children. Marina was never good at housework, and didn't like it. There was no telephone, so they had no news from the hospital. Everyone was worried. When the family went to meet the bus from the hospital early one morning, Marina was still sweeping the kitchen, wanting to have everything finished to satisfy her mother. She believed she would soon see her parents and sisters coming up the road.

But when her father and sisters arrived, they were crying. Marina knew then that her mother had died, but no tears came. She has cried with grief for her mother many times since, but at the time it happened, she was the strong one.

Marina comforted her sisters. No one else in her family could do anything. She cooked and made her younger sisters eat. Her father was devastated with grief. Marina took care of everyone.

Marina's sister De Deusa had recently been married. When De Deusa returned to her own home, she left Marina in charge of the house and younger children. Life was always such a struggle, so much hard work, and things got no better. Now she and her father struggled against grief also. They knew that their hard work and prayers must strengthen them to carry on. This was the *nordestino* way, to hang on no matter how bitter life became, to continue to work, pray, and hope for better times. The family never gave up their strong principles of honesty and hard work.

Marina had to care for six children, the house, and the garden. It was hard work and a lot of responsibility. And soon Marina was not well herself: now she had hepatitis.

Hepatitis is a serious disease of the liver causing exhaustion, drowsiness, fever, nausea, and loss of

This rubber tapper family stands in front of their house in Acre, Marina Silva's home state. Their house is raised on stilts to keep water out— much like Marina's was. The couple's children are still young, but soon the older two will be able to help with gardening, cooking, and even collecting sap.

appetite. It can cause death. Common causes of hepatitis in Amazonia are polluted water and poisoning from malaria medicine.

Marina spent months struggling to live, while still trying to help her family whenever and however she could. As she lay in her hammock day after day, she contemplated her life. Was this her destiny—clinging onto an existence of work, disease, and death? If she had children, would this be their fate, too? It didn't seem right to her. This wasn't the work she felt God had brought her into the world to do. But she knew so little of the world beyond the forest—how could she know?

She longed to become a nun. To be a nun would build her character and identity in the *nordestino* tradition, like her father: strong, honest, courageous, and persevering in the face of generations of intense hardship and death. As a nun, she would have a relationship with God that made sense of such suffering.

This wasn't the only time Marina had thought of becoming a nun. She'd first had this dream as a child, while sleeping in her grandmother's hut. Together, Marina and her grandmother had recited prayers until Marina knew them all. A life of devotion and prayer appealed to her strong spirit. But to be a nun required years of study, reading, and writing. How ridiculous, she thought, to hope that such a ragged, illiterate forest girl could become a nun!

Yet, in the city, in Rio Branco, she could get treatment for hepatitis, and perhaps she could go to a Catholic school. They were the best schools in Brazil. She would learn to read and write, learn about God and the world, and answer the questions burning

Collecting fruit from the trees in the rainforest is a job often done by children, and is a great source of vitamins in a family's diet. Fruit and nuts are a renewable source of food for families living in the rainforest, because harvesting doesn't hurt the trees.

From above, the rainforest of Acre extends as far as the eye can see. The small clearing in the lower left is a rubber tapper village. Only this small area needs to be cleared in the forest to support several families.

within her. Surely a Catholic school would prepare her to be a nun—if only she could go!

She worked up her courage for a month before she asked her father. "I didn't think he would let me," she later said. She was the oldest; how would he get along without her? Marina whispered her wish "more to myself than to him," she recalled.

To her astonishment, her father agreed. "This is what you want? Then it's all right," he said calmly. "Do you want to go this week or next? Maybe next. I'm going to sell some rubber this week, so at least you can go with something in your pocket."

Family is very important in Brazil. People call even distant relations "cousins." Marina's family was very close. For her to go to the city was exciting to some, frightening to others. Her grandfather was against it. "If her mother was alive she would never have allowed it," he insisted. But Marina and her father won out.

Though not a big city, Rio Branco seemed huge and strange to Marina. Unpainted houses, shops, and bars lined the unpaved streets for blocks. Vendors sold food and trinkets laid out in bowls or hung from their wooden carts. Brazil's many kinds of music blasted from every shop and bar.

People, mostly poor, crowded everywhere. Few wore shoes or nice clothes. Men and boys went shirtless, often only in swim trunks. By the river, people and dogs picked through trash piles for food. Soldiers and military police with guns patrolled in jeeps, while cars, trucks, and buses struggled through the mud.

In the central plaza, the grand cathedral, police headquarters, and government buildings towered over her. Marina had never experienced electricity on such a large scale. "I still remember," she said years later,

Why is education rare in Brazil?

Most people in Brazil attend school for just a few years. Millions of people are too poor to go to school. Hungry families don't have money for bus fare, uniforms, paper, pencils, and books, and children drop out to work. They don't learn to read well, and later can't help their own children learn. Still, most parents value education and try to get as much as they can for their children. But many places have no school at all. Many public schools are in sad condition, with leaky roofs and broken toilets. Teachers' pay is very low, less than $200 a month, so few people take the job. Often teachers have only passed fourth grade themselves.

The result is that almost a third of Brazilians cannot read newspapers, and twenty-three million cannot write their names. Less than a quarter of children who start school make it to eighth grade, one of the worst drop-out rates in the world. Yet Brazil spends only a third of its education budget on elementary schools, much less than most countries.

Most families that can afford it pay for private Catholic schooling. Only the Catholic schools prepare students for the difficult college entrance exams, so most university students come from upper and middle class families.

"the amazement I felt seeing Christmas trees decorated with fairy lights." She was just sixteen, and she had changed her life.

She stayed at first with a cousin, then with an uncle, while getting treatment at a free Catholic hospital. As she felt better, she found a job as a maid. She started school at an evening program for poor adults sponsored by the Brazilian Literacy Movement.

After only two weeks, Marina had learned to read and write. She remembered, "My teacher said that I learned too fast." She was sent to a special program. "There it was possible to complete the four years of primary school in just one year." Though she started the course near the end of the term, she was one of only three students who passed in the class of forty-six.

She had proved to others—and herself—that she could learn. Her dream *was* possible. Marina found a convent that ran a school and would let her in. At

Rio Branco, the capital of the state of Acre, is a medium sized city, not far from the border with Bolivia. Of its 229,000 people, some are very rich, but many are poor and live on the streets or in shacks in slums called favelas.

first, the sister in charge doubted Marina could catch up. They said she could drop back a grade if she had to. But she not only caught up, she did so well that they let her skip the final exams.

Living at the convent was everything Marina had hoped. The chores and strict schedule weren't difficult for a former *seringueira*. Quiet and prayer were soothing after the past years of struggle and grief. Most of all, Marina took great joy in writing, learning, and especially reading.

The next year she finished sixth grade, and also passed the exams to enter high school. She was pleased, but later wrote, "I thought I still had a lot to learn. I didn't know Portuguese grammar well enough, or mathematics, and I lacked a foreign language." All this was necessary to qualify for the university entrance exams. No one expected the miracle of the poor rubber tapper girl to continue, except Marina herself.

But her goals were changing. Although she liked the convent's religious life, it wasn't right for her. At nineteen years old, Marina was just discovering life's possibilities. Becoming a nun no longer appealed to her the way it had in the forest. She thought now of marriage, and of having children whose lives could be different. And beyond her own satisfaction, she thought about what she could accomplish for others. Most of all, she wanted a better life for the *seringueiros* and other forest peoples.

She remembered, "Months before I was to be initiated as a nun, I told them that I wasn't going to become a nun anymore. I had acquired a strong notion of justice."

Chapter 4
THE AMAZON IS BURNING

While Marina was going to school in Rio Branco, change swept Acre. Ranchers forced families from their homes and land, where they had lived for generations. Hundreds of thousands of acres of rainforest were burned, destroying Brazil nut, rubber, and many other valuable trees. Countless species of plants and animals, both known and undiscovered, were lost. At the World Bank, which lent Brazil the money for the development projects, one consultant called the devastation "more widespread and more lasting than that caused by a hurricane or an earthquake. But instead of receiving aid for disaster relief, Brazil is expected to pay the World Bank for helping make the disaster happen."

Homeless families flocked to the city but found no work, no housing, no food, no relief programs. Marina remembered the horror: "To see families that lived in the forest with dignity, in the *favelas,* in terrible poverty—it was a great motivation to become involved in political work, in social movements."

Just as many trees make a forest, many people make a movement. All over Brazil, people joined movements, including Christian base communities (CBCs), to create change. There were over 80,000 CBCs in Brazil. Workers formed unions to demand fair treatment. Priests, nuns, and union activists organized landless farmers to claim unused land. In Acre, the actions called *empates* (em-POTCH-ayz)

Rio de Janeiro, once the capital of Brazil, is a city of over six million people. It is a city of expensive apartments and luxurious houses as well as favelas *like this one, where people displaced from farms or the forest make homes out of scrap building materials.*

What is a *favela*?

Favela is the Portuguese word for slum. Every city in Brazil has its *favela*, and big cities have many. *Favelas* began when poor people without land came to the cities looking for work. With nowhere to live and little or no money, they built shacks from scraps of lumber, metal, or cardboard on empty land.

Favelas often have no streets, sewers, garbage removal, plumbing, schools, or health care. Water must be carried home from public taps. Drug dealers are often the community bosses, paying for services like waste collection and electricity in return for cooperation and secrecy.

Most people living in *favelas*, even small children, work for the little pay they can get. Food is expensive, and millions are always hungry. Many children don't earn enough to get home every day, so they live and sleep on the streets.

People who are better off often react angrily to *favelados*. Police evict them and bulldoze their shacks, or make arrests for no reason. Business owners sometimes hire off-duty police officers to round up street children and beat or kill them. Some people try to improve life for *favelados*—priests, nuns, teachers, activists, and government officials—but often they are threatened and even murdered.

were organized by *seringueiros* to save their land. *Empate* is a Portuguese word meaning "standoff." The first *empate* took place in 1976, when Wilson Pinheiro got a group together to prevent the clearing of a *seringueiro's* land. Many of the people taking part in *empates* were also members of CBCs and unions.

Marina joined *empates* organized by Chico Mendes, a well-known union activist. Many times Marina crowded with dozens of people into trucks for the ride through the forest. After bouncing for hours over dirt roads, they hiked through the rainforest to the scene of the *empate*. As they went they sang old songs from the northeast—songs about the forest and their life, songs of inspiration for their struggle.

When they crossed cleared land, Marina felt the

destruction through her whole body. The sun hammered down on tough grass, foul weeds, thornbushes, and earth baked brick hard. Burrs and briars stuck to their clothes. Marina felt as though the land was sick.

Sweat poured from their bodies in the heat. If a rainstorm caught them in the open, they ran for the trees. Treacherous rivers of mud that formed instantly sent them sliding. The tortured ground couldn't soak up rain. When she reentered the forest, Marina felt relieved. The pounding rain became a gentle patter high overhead. The tall forest was cool, clean, calm, alive.

The cries of monkeys and birds, the chirps and clicks of frogs and beetles were soon drowned out by the angry whine of chain saws. Giant, century-old trees toppled, thrashing through smaller trees to slam to the ground. Marina and the rubber tappers exchanged glances full of pain: Was that a rubber tree? Brazil nut tree? A tree useful to people?

The work crew stopped when they saw the *seringueiros* approach. The workers stood in a line,

Marina leads an empate *to stop loggers clearing a patch of forest.* Empates *are a face to face, nonviolent way to prevent destruction of rainforest communities. Sometimes tree cutting was stopped, and sometimes the protestors were arrested or hurt, but the* empates *got the attention of reporters and audiences around the world, which helps to stop deforestation.* Empates *still take place today, as the forest is constantly threatened.*

To make way for ranches and farms, huge swaths of rainforest are burned. This is considered the fastest way to get rid of the dense forest plants, vines, and trees, although it also destroys valuable sources of timber, food, rubber, medicines, animal habitat, and people's livelihoods.

blocking the path, some holding their guns ready. The ranchers hated *empates*. They often sent gunmen along with the work crews to frighten away *seringueiros*.

The *serirgueiros* stopped, and Chico spoke to the workers. "Don't be nervous. We don't have guns!" he called. "We're not here to fight."

The workers still held their guns. "Go away," their leader shouted. "We have orders to fire."

Chico introduced himself to the young, nervous gunmen. Chico explained that *seringueiros* and the work crew were alike. "You're a worker, like us." Chico explained how much they all had in common. They talked about the families living on this land, people just like the crew's families.

"The ranchers' aim is to get everything," Chico went on. "They'll destroy the natural wealth which belongs to *seringueiros*, to you, and all workers. It'll be great for the ranchers; everywhere will be fenced and full of cattle. Then how will we live?"

As they talked, the crew grew less tense. The crew leader told them why he took this terrible job: the landowner forced him off the plot of land he farmed.

Marina and the other *seringueiros* nodded. They had heard many stories like his. Chico asked, "Why shouldn't the poor defend themselves from the rich? We are from this rainforest. We don't want you to be expelled. You were born in the same place as your father and your grandfather. Just because some rich guy from the south comes and says the land is his, you let him have it? What are you thinking?"

The workers *were* thinking. Rich landowners were the enemy, not the *seringueiros*. The *empates* fought for all of them against the way the ranchers pushed them around. The leader of the work crew signaled for his men to come and talk it over.

The crew agreed to leave. Chico hopped with delight, and the *seringueiros* smiled at their success. The *empate* ended peacefully.

Not every *empate* succeeded. Sometimes work crews ignored the tappers. When the protesters joined hands to block the saws and bulldozers, people sometimes got hurt. It was hard for the *seringueiros* to stay peaceful. They were beaten, kicked, even shot and killed. Yet *empates* were saving the forest. The *seringueiros* had faith in the justice of their cause. Their belief in the morality of nonviolence helped them withstand the harsh treatment.

Marina was one of the first women to join *empates*. More women, and children, too, followed. Having women and children in the group showed the work crews and hired police that the *seringueiros* didn't want violence.

The *seringueiros'* solidarity impressed workers throughout Brazil. They too wanted land, a good livelihood, and a healthy, peaceful future for their children.

What is solidarity?

Solidarity is standing up for others the way you would stand up for a friend. It comes from understanding that what affects some people affects everyone. Solidarity is people acting together because the needs of some matter to all. For example, teachers in one town may go on strike to support teachers on strike in another town. Even though the teachers in the first town are happy with their jobs, they take a stand in solidarity with teachers in the other who face problems.

Solidarity expresses the understanding that people cannot be truly happy and free while others are suffering and oppressed.

Burning the forest left the soil stripped of minerals needed to grow healthy crops. Without the roots of thousands of plants, the soil couldn't hold in water. Rain stood in muddy puddles in low places, or ran off in streams. The dry soil blew away, leaving a desert waste.

Marina felt inspired by the *empates* and movements for social justice. When she joined, she felt she was at the very bottom, just a poor, ignorant girl, a lowly *seringueira*. She thought she needed a lot more confidence before she could be anything like Chico Mendes and Wilson Pinheiro. She gained that confidence, and, in years to come, organized and led *empates* herself.

While Marina went to school and *empates,* she was also involved with CBCs. Here she learned about liberation theology and the methods of Brazil's world-famous educator Paulo Freire.

Freire saw that people's life situations shaped their attitudes and ability to learn. People who are not treated as worthwhile by society may not think of themselves as worthwhile. They often believe a worthless person can't learn to read and write. When they grasp that they do have abilities, their outlook on life changes. They are empowered. Freire developed teaching methods that would help empower people, especially poor people.

CBCs combined Freire's methods with liberation theology, which is based on Jesus' teachings about human rights and dignity. Liberation theology showed Marina how her burning need to understand God, herself, and the world was connected to her life of hardship. Her grandmother's simple morals expanded into a vision of justice and equality.

CBCs empower people to overcome hopelessness about their lives. Meeting several times each week, students and teachers together question their situations, and connect their own lives to the teachings of Jesus.

Marina thought in new ways about her own life. She questioned everything: where and how she lived, where she could and couldn't go, her relations with men and women of all social levels, what she knew and didn't know. Thinking about these things helped her understand the injustice of *seringuieros'* place in Brazil, and why she must work to change it.

CBCs support equality for women, at home and in society. Marina did a man's work as a girl, and had a flexible attitude about women's place in society. Her CBC encouraged her ideas about her own life to broaden. Her concerns now included humanity, the forest, and Brazil. She began to think of herself as more than just a poor girl toiling and praying alone.

She lived, learned, and taught others in an atmosphere of constant questioning and empowerment. Historical figures like St. Francis of Assisi and Gandhi of India became her role models. These men acted politically against tremendous odds. Their deep religious convictions created lasting change. Like them, the shy woman from the forest was now empowered with a deep sense of justice.

What are Christian base communities and liberation theology?

The Catholic Church started Christian base communities in the 1960s to help poor Latin Americans out of extreme poverty.

Theology means study of God and religion. The thoughts and writing of priests living among the poor of Latin America created the theology of liberation. They believe that true Christians must work together to improve the world for all people, just as Jesus did. This is a major force for change in Latin America.

Liberation theologists criticize Church history. They believe that instead of working to create a just and peaceful world, the Church has too often supported the rich and powerful, while teaching the poor that they should suffer patiently in their lives for their reward in heaven. CBCs encourage people to work to better their lives now.

Hundreds of homeless families march to protest government policies that pushed them off their farms and seringals. A huge number of people can live in slums, segregated from a city, without the world paying attention to their situation, but demonstrations like this one show how big and desperate the homeless population is.

A young man named Raimundo Gomes de Souza lived near Marina and went to both her church and her school. Marina first noticed him because he seemed lonely and shy. She thought he should have someone to talk to. Soon, they talked the whole way to school.

Raimundo was in his last year of high school as Marina was beginning there. Both were poor, and Raimundo's father had died, so Marina felt they had much in common. He too wanted to go to college. She felt a strong connection to him.

Marina became parish coordinator for their church. Raimundo made posters and helped Marina organize her first demonstration, "The March of the Excluded Ones," to get water and electric lights for the *favelados* of Rio Branco.

She spent more and more time with Raimundo, and they grew closer. Soon he asked Marina to marry him, and she accepted. But they were not to be married just yet.

In the midst of her political activities, Marina had done what most Brazilians only dream of—finished high school. At the age of twenty, she began studying for the difficult university entrance exams. So shy as a girl, she was now knowledgeable and less afraid to speak out. The entrance exams, given once each year, were coming soon. She didn't want to miss them.

But illness struck again: another kind of hepatitis. There was no treatment in Rio Branco; she had to go to the technological center of Brazil, São Paulo. Her friend, the Bishop of Rio Branco, helped her arrange treatment. Her father and uncles used their savings to pay for the trip of over 2,000 kilometers to the south.

Chapter 5

"A STRONG NOTION OF JUSTICE"

On her way to São Paulo, Marina flew over the rainforest for the first time. Trees stretched as far as she could see. Storm clouds released rain. But swaths of brown cut the rainforest short. Roads, ranches, and farms chewed their way into Amazonia's heart. Development was like a cancer, turning life into death.

In São Paulo, she saw a truly modern city for the first time, the third largest in the world. Well-dressed people, new cars, and tourists crowded the streets. A stone's throw from the skyscrapers, millions suffered in *favelas*. During her three months of treatment, she saw poor patients lying in the hospital halls. Many died without seeing a doctor.

Marina missed the university entrance exams that year. When she returned to Rio Branco, Raimundo had just finished a training course with the National Electric Company. They married, the fulfillment of one of Marina's dreams: to have a family of her own.

The following year, expecting her first child, Marina passed the exams with an excellent score. Only four years earlier she couldn't read or write. Now she would enter the Federal College of History in Rio Branco.

All her life, Marina asked questions. At the university, she found some answers. To her delight, she discovered many books by people who thought as she did about freedom and equality for all. Most of the other students had grown up with opportunities

Marina spoke about protecting the rainforest and forest communities to church groups, audiences of street theater, and workers who lived on the seringal *and in the city. She also helped workers join together in unions to protect their work and homes.*

Marina never had. Talking with them increased her confidence and helped her express herself.

University tuition was free, but students provided their own living expenses. Marina worked at two jobs. One was at a shelter for homeless children. The other was a night job sewing clothes. These two jobs paid very little, and she and Raimundo often could not meet their expenses.

It was difficult for Marina to do so much, and she needed to take care of her health and her pregnancy. But she could not put aside her goals. *Empates* and other activities were as important as her family. She worked hard for a better future for her children. Her daughter Shalon was born in 1981.

An area of rainforest bigger than the state of Massachusetts was cleared and burned every year, and nothing stood in the way of the chain saws but the *seringueiros*. The rest of the world didn't seem to notice or care. "We felt so insignificant at times," Marina remembers. "We wondered if anyone was listening to us."

A very large *empate* was organized at Boca do Acre. Hundreds of families came, many traveling over 400 kilometers on foot and by boat. The work crew fled. It was a victory for the *seringueiros*. But the ranchers were very angry. Officials and priests encouraged the *seringueiros* to leave and avoid violence.

Wilson Pinheiro pointed out that the money, jobs, or small plots of land the ranchers offered the *seringueiros* would only allow a family to live for a short while. Then what? They'd end up in the *favela*. The *seringueiros* knew Wilson spoke the truth. They refused to give in. This angered the ranchers even

Wilson Pinheiro helped found the Rural Workers Union to protect seringueiros, *and led the first* empate *in Brazil. This poster showing him with one of his children was made after he was assassinated by ranchers in 1980.*

more. They saw Wilson as a troublemaker. No one understood the *seringuieros'* love for the forest.

After generations of believing they had no rights, the *seringueiros* finally formed their own union, Sindicato de Trabalhadores Rurais, the Rural Workers Union. Starting unions was dangerous. Union leaders were arrested, tortured, or killed. In 1979, angry ranchers had hired men to beat Chico Mendes. The *seringueiros'* struggle seemed hopeless to others. A rancher told Chico, "You against us is like a mosquito against a lion."

What are human rights?

Human rights are those rights that belong to all human beings. The right to life itself and the basic necessities of food and clothing are considered to be fundamental human rights. But the definition of human rights has broadened in the nineteenth and twentieth centuries. Human rights now make up three categories of rights for all people: individual rights, social rights, and collective rights.

Individual rights are the rights to life, liberty, privacy, the security of the individual, freedom of speech and press, freedom of worship, the right to own property, freedom from slavery, freedom from torture and unusual punishment, and similar rights, including those that are spelled out in the first ten amendments to the Constitution of the United States. Individual rights are based on the idea that the government should shield its citizens from any violations of these rights.

Social rights demand that governments provide such things as quality education, jobs, adequate medical care, housing, and other benefits. Basically, they call for a standard of living adequate for the health and well-being of the citizens of every nation.

Collective rights were spelled out in a document called the Universal Declaration of Human Rights, which was adopted by the General Assembly of the United Nations on December 10, 1948. This document proclaims the right of all human beings in the world to political, economic, social, and cultural self-determination; the right to peace; the right to live in a healthful and balanced environment; and the right to share in the earth's resources. The Universal Declaration of Human Rights also pledges the rights of life, liberty, and security of person—the basic individual human rights.

The next year, Wilson Pinheiro was assassinated. Wilson's murder was not even investigated. Officials in Acre—mayors, police, judges, lawyers—were friends of the ranchers. A group of hurt, angry *seringueiros* avenged Wilson's death by killing a rancher. Within a day, hundreds of *seringueiros* were arrested and tortured.

Though the regime had loosened some of its controls, soldiers and military police patrolled the streets, and arrests and torture were still common. People were afraid to speak out, though oppression and Brazil's bad economy had made the majority of Brazilians eager for change.

Marina acted in a street theater group that drew attention to oppression. She joined a student group opposed to the regime, led by a member of a new political party, Partido dos Trabalhadores (PT), the Workers' Party. When the regime legalized political parties, many quickly sprang up. But only the PT welcomed *seringueiros,* indigenous people, landless

Police arrest a homeless man. Conflict broke out between the military regime and the hundreds of thousands of people who were made homeless by the government's development projects. Desperate, hungry people marched and protested peacefully, and police began making arrests. Friends or relatives might be taken away and return hurt or beaten, or not return at all.

farmers, and others excluded from power and opportunity. PT rules require that at least 30 percent of party positions be held by women. Marina decided to join the PT.

Chico Mendes was involved in the PT, and was running in the new elections. Marina wanted to work with him. He was changing Amazonia. She could learn a lot and help her people by helping Chico. She ran his election campaign for state representative with the help of her student group.

In Brazilian politics people feel they "owe" someone their vote, regardless of whether the candidate would improve their lives. A typical candidate reminds everyone of this "debt," and gives away money or food to make the point. In Acre, where many people were voting for the first time, the ranchers' candidates gave away pressure cookers, chain saws, shirts, and other things in exchange for votes. These proved the candidate was rich. Money won elections. People thought that voting for

Unions bring together people who do similar work to bargain for fair working conditions and fair pay. Here union members gather to vote on important decisions, such as holding an empate or a strike, accepting a work contract at a rubber or coffee estate, or seeking more just labor laws.

Marina meets with church leaders and seringueiros *to talk about illegal logging. Bringing together people from all parts of the community to talk about a problem makes better solutions than excluding local people from making decisions and legislation.*

someone who couldn't win was "wasting your vote." People thought Chico couldn't win, so they didn't vote for him.

Rich candidates made fabulous promises that made the future sound like a television show: refrigerators, cars, fancy clothes. People liked to hope: maybe *this* politician isn't lying *this* time—especially if he was handsome and looked upper class like a television star. They found out later he was lying.

Chico and Marina wanted to change the way things worked. They knew there was no democracy when the richest candidate won. They wanted to get votes by talking about issues. They spoke about the difficult struggle ahead, but this reminded people of how bad things were. Chico lost the election.

But the *seringueiro* movement was growing. The Rural Workers Union organized cooperatives to buy and sell rubber and supplies at fair prices. The union built schools, and Marina helped train teachers. Her dream of education could come true for others.

It is very hard for uneducated people to fully participate in government. Government makes laws and appoints officials and judges. Without government positions, how could *seringueiros* get beyond fighting with ranchers in the forest? Education for Amazonia's poor meant a future of greater citizenship.

There was exciting talk of a presidential election in the future. Luís Inácio Lula da Silva, known as Lula, would be the PT's candidate. One of eight children of poor, landless farmers, Lula had worked from the age of seven to help feed his family. At the end of the 1970s he led São Paulo's autoworkers in strikes that gave unions new power against the regime. Three times he has almost been elected president.

Lula was proof that poor workers with little schooling were able to enter Brazil's highest offices.

Marina and Chico started a branch of the PT in Acre. They also founded a branch of CUT, the Central Workers Union. CUT linked unions across Brazil, thereby connecting Acre's unions with workers in other states. More people would hear about *empates* and the *seringueiros'* struggle for justice. It seemed that Marina, Chico, and their activist friends worked twenty-four hours a day.

Chico Mendes was a close friend to Marina. The hours Marina spent with Chico in the forest and in their office in Xapuri (shap-poor-EE) continued her education. She learned about politics and Brazil's history of struggle for equality. Chico, like Marina, was committed to nonviolence. Sharing the ideas of people like Mahatma Gandhi and Martin Luther King, Jr., they agreed that violence only brings more violence.

Chico's warmth and sincerity won him the trust of the *seringueiro* community. He listened to everyone, never treating some people as more important than others. His gentle, dark eyes and friendly personality made him easy to talk to. But he was not soft-spoken when standing up for the *seringueiros*. He was angry at the ranchers and the government, and he didn't back down. "The most important thing I learned from him was commitment," Marina later said. "Chico always knew that he could die for what he was defending."

Marina, Chico, and the other union organizers knew they could become targets, as Wilson had. But the only way to stop murders and terror for good was to keep working for justice.

A rural leader murdered in a conflict over land ownership is carried home by friends and coworkers. Ranchers who wanted more land to clear for raising cattle also had money for guns, hired thugs, and bribes for officials and the police. Often they got away with murdering people who defended the land they lived on.

What is the history of nonviolent resistance?

For centuries people have used nonviolent tactics to fight for their rights, tactics such as boycotts (refusing to buy anything from an unjust government or company), huge public meetings and marches, labor strikes (refusing to work), hunger strikes (refusing to eat), or noncooperation (refusing to obey unjust laws). Nonviolent resistance may look weak, but when enough people refuse to go along with injustice, the government is almost helpless.

Mahatma Gandhi led millions of Indians in boycotts, strikes, marches, and fasts that showed England that it couldn't rule India. Gandhi's deep spiritual beliefs gave him commitment to nonviolent action. Likewise, Reverend Dr. Martin Luther King, Jr., chose nonviolence during the American Civil Rights Movement of the 1950s and 1960s, leading voter-registration campaigns, peaceful law breaking, and the famous bus boycotts against racial segregation. The cruelty and racism of officials who sent the police, with clubs, dogs, and tear gas, against unarmed marchers shocked the world. Right now in Burma, Aung San Suu Kyi protests against the military regime with letter-writing campaigns while she is held under house arrest.

In addition to leaders, nonviolence must have the commitment of many heroic, unknown people to succeed. Back in the 1770s American colonists fought English rule with boycotts of British tea and sugar. In the 1800s and early 1900s women in America, England, and around the world marched and went on hunger strikes to win the right to vote. Before the Civil War people in the United States hid African Americans escaping to freedom on the Underground Railroad. Widespread noncooperation with Nazi orders saved Jews in Norway, Belgium, Denmark, and Bulgaria from death camps. Workers everywhere have used labor strikes to improve safety and fairness at their jobs. In U.S. cities, groups of mothers have organized nighttime marches to chase gangs and drug dealers out of their neighborhoods. The dedication to justice of so many people inspires human rights movements around the world.

Justice was in short supply. Across Brazil, poor people were being killed in land conflicts. None of these murders were investigated. The poor courageously continued protesting, having chosen between misery if they did nothing, or a chance at a decent life if they survived.

All her life, Marina had felt the suffering of her

family and their trees. Now she felt the misery of all the people and trees of Acre. Her personal family had grown also, with the birth of a son, Danilo, in 1982.

Her university studies, jobs, and political work often took her away from Raimundo and their two babies. While she was a student, she worked as a teacher in the convent and in a public school. She felt guilty leaving her children so often, and missing them as they grew. Raimundo's mother and Marina's Aunt Chica took care of them. It made Marina jealous to hear her children calling her Aunt Chica "Mom." She wondered if they would grow up confused, or hate her for being away so much.

Though it tore her heart, Marina knew what she was doing was right; her work created a better world for her children. She was grateful for Aunt Chica and Raimundo's mother.

Women at the university judged her. They couldn't understand how a married mother of two could be

Women's groups have become more and more important in Brazil. Working together makes women aware of their strength and organizing power. Women's movements in Brazil take on environmental and reproduction issues, organize unions, work for human rights, and are a force in politics. Women's groups in favelas *also organize for clean water, healthcare, and other basic services.*

studying and involved in so many activities. They called Marina a bad mother. This was very painful. Marina loved her children deeply. How could people think this of her?

There is tremendous reverence for life in the rainforest. The wives of the first, exhausted *seringueiros* transformed their huts into lively homes with children, gardens, and animals. For Marina to be thought a bad mother went beyond judging her treatment of her children; it implied an uncaring attitude toward women's nurturing of the community, society, and the life of the planet. This was deeply wounding to her.

What does equality mean for women in Brazil?

Historically, in Brazil as elsewhere, women were considered inferior to men and were viewed as their possessions. Early rubber tappers could order a wife from the boss, along with other supplies. When a man was hired to do farm work the boss assumed his wife would also work, but without pay. A husband was entitled by Brazilian law to beat or murder his wife or daughters to preserve his "honor."

Some things are slow to change. Most work is still different for women and men, and "women's work" still earns lower pay or none at all. In 1980 in São Paulo, 772 women were murdered by their husbands, but none of the men were punished.

But women's groups in Brazil's cities are working hard to end domestic violence, to get better education for more women, and to get women into more influential and high-paying jobs at pay equal to men. Brazil's women's groups are considered the largest and most effective in Latin America. Since 1990, many more women are completing high school and college than ever before, and becoming lawyers, professors, journalists, politicians, and doctors. Still, though more than half the lawyers in Brazil's Bar Association are women, there is not a single woman on the board of directors.

Fighting for their rights and speaking their views gives women a new sense of themselves, often leading to conflict at home. Some men forbid women from going to meetings, but some men support their wives' or daughters' work by taking care of children and learning to share housework.

Marina's reading in psychology, especially books by Erich Fromm, helped her understand this painful time. She saw that people could enslave themselves to a familiar role, like Mother or Father, and a set of traditional activities and ideas, rather than choose their own path.

"Women's rights, be it in the most luxurious neighborhoods of São Paulo or in the *seringals,* are not respected," Marina later wrote. She gained understanding of her feelings. "I love my children and all people, but above all, I love humanity. How could I close myself from the world, where families are losing their land and going hungry all around me?"

Most Brazilian men also felt a wife's place was at home. Raimundo didn't like Marina's activities. He stopped taking part in CBC work, and missed experiences that raised Marina's awareness and strengthened her commitment.

In order to continue the struggle for justice, Marina would face some difficult choices.

Chapter 6

"FIRST THE DREAM, THEN THE FIGHT"

Marina's dedication to social justice grew, but Raimundo's ideas about their family were more traditional. Though they had shared religious and political work when they were younger, they no longer did. Marina had already overcome criticism from other women. It felt at times as though she were being crushed by other people's ideas and expectations of her as a woman, wife, and mother. Marina fought every day for workers' right to the life they chose; why shouldn't women have the same right? She couldn't go on this way.

It was agonizing to let go of their marriage. Marina and Raimundo had two children. Her upbringing gave her a strong sense of honor and commitment. But she could not give up her work for humanity—not for anyone or anything. She separated from Raimundo in 1985, a year after she graduated from college.

Marina became the coordinator of CUT, the Central Workers Union of Acre, in Rio Branco. While Chico walked from house to house in the forest, Marina worked in the towns and in Rio Branco, teaching and talking with people about the struggle, unions, *empates,* and the rainforest.

People listened. Marina was a passionate, articulate speaker. She was also the rubber tapper girl who went to college—the dream walking around for everyone to see that *it could be done.* Her energy gave the poor of Acre hope.

Since becoming a senator, Marina travels each year to other countries to speak about the rainforest, the people living in it, and the future of our planet.

By now, the *seringueiros* weren't the only people trying to save the rainforest. Journalists, scholars, indigenous leaders, and activists from all over Brazil and from other countries heard about the burning and came to Acre. Anthropologists who came to study indigenous people worried about the future of the rainforest communities. Environmentalists were concerned about the destruction of the rainforest's unique ecosystem. Some of these experts sought out Chico and offered their help. They helped *seringueiros,* indigenous leaders, unions, and government officials all talk together for the first time. Suddenly, *seringueiros* found out what rainforest destruction meant to the rest of the world.

Though Marina had never heard the word "ecology" before, she understood immediately what it meant. She was raised as an ecologist, an expert on the rainforest ecosystem. Ecology was a way to defend the forest that the world paid attention to.

What is sustainable development?

Development replaces natural environments with human ones in order to make money and improve lives. Most development plans try to copy the way the United States, Europe, and Japan became rich and modern through large-scale farming, mining, power production, and technology building. Unfortunately, that kind of development used up, or exploited, natural resources and destroyed the environment. Those countries then looked elsewhere for more resources to exploit in order to keep making money, building dams for power plants, drilling for oil, or clearing land for roads, ranches, and farms.

These development projects around the world destroy ecosystems, drive millions from their homes, and wipe out or scatter indigenous peoples. The rich make money while the poor grow even poorer, ripping societies apart with violence, crime, and injustice.

Sustainable development works *with* nature, instead of destroying nature, helping people make a living without destroying the ecosystem. For instance, people who gather rainforest resources might get equipment to make finished products themselves; then the money from local resources goes to local people who care for the environment, instead of to distant business owners. Careful logging and local furniture making keep the forest healthy, provide local jobs, and earn more money than just selling lumber would. Other sustainable development projects include making art and handicrafts, rubber tapping, and gathering wild foods.

Environmental groups sprang up in Brazil. Thousands of citizens in other countries protested rainforest destruction. The PT put environmental issues on its platform.

The *seringueiros* came up with a new way to protect the rainforest, called extractive reserves. Extractive reserves were large areas of land set aside for people who extract their livelihood from the forest by gathering rubber, Brazil nuts, and other forest products. Rainforest plants and animals would be protected from ranchers, loggers, poachers, mining prospectors, and settlers, and the *seringueiros'* way of life would improve.

While Chico worked out this idea with indigenous leaders, environmentalists, and anthropologists, Marina ran Chico's campaign for mayor in Xapuri and talked over the idea with the people she met. While campaigning, Marina described extractive reserves as the solution to Acre's problem: a way to fight poverty and hunger, and make a better quality of life without destroying the rainforest.

The government's plans for development didn't work, but Marina knew development would happen no matter what. Acre needed schools, roads, and hospitals. With government support, extractive reserves could provide those services. Marina was committed to getting *seringueiros* into the government, and Chico was their strongest leader.

A new organization, the National Council of Seringueiros, proposed extractive reserves to the government. The response was positive. But Brazil's government is notoriously slow. It often makes promises to look good and then goes back on them.

Chico Mendes and his family stand outside the headquarters of the Rural Workers Union in Xapuri, where he worked to organize rubber tappers. The union became a powerful force for protecting the forest and representing Brazil's poor.

Marina felt extractive reserves must not be allowed to falter. Only the government could create reserves. How could *seringueiros* make it happen?

Many politicians saw their office as a way to gain wealth and status. They weren't interested in improving things for others. When the people who make laws are dishonest and greedy, powerless people suffer.

Only acting together—voting together—gave the poor power. Marina recalled, "I finally realized that in all the social fights I was carrying on, trying to give the people from the Amazon better lives, and in making this region self-sufficient without spoiling the Amazon, that I needed government action, not only social and nongovernment movements." With Chico's urging, she shyly agreed to run for office herself.

At the next election her picture was beside Chico's on the PT poster. She ran for federal, and Chico for

How does the fate of the rainforest affect the global environment?

Everything that burns in a power plant, car engine, furnace, or forest fire makes carbon dioxide, which traps the earth's heat. This is called global warming. Between 5 and 20 percent of all the carbon dioxide released each year comes from burning the Amazon rainforest.

Global warming is causing the earth's climate to change. Too much or too little rain ruins crops and causes drought or floods. Hurricanes are more frequent and violent. Seasons are too hot or too cold, changing plant and insect life cycles, affecting birds, animals, and people. Coasts are flooded as the oceans rise.

Amazonia affects weather on the whole planet in ways scientists don't fully understand. The fate of Amazonia is more important to the rest of the world than any other region on the planet.

state representative for Acre. Though they didn't get enough votes to win, Marina was a popular candidate. This was encouraging for a young, poor candidate in a new party. Her hard work was making a difference.

Politicians are usually from the large, wealthy families that have run Brazil for 500 years. Descended from colonial plantation owners, they expect to run against other elite men like themselves. Their politics are much the same. The difference is who will benefit from their election—which friends and families will get government jobs, and who will hear about land and business deals.

These powerful men expect to crush opponents like Marina and Chico, and usually do. The PT didn't have money for publicity, or friends who owned newspapers, radio, and television stations. The PT didn't believe in buying votes or making promises they wouldn't keep. People thought the PT didn't have a chance.

They lost that election, but Marina identified the problem: not enough people understood the issues. She set about making sure that everyone in Acre, not just *seringueiros* and indigenous people, understood sustainable development and extractive reserves.

She quoted from studies that proved collecting rubber and Brazil nuts made twenty times more money from the same amount of Amazon land than either farms or ranches. This was a surprise; most people assumed the opposite. Most people had thought little money could come from the forest because the *seringueiros* were always poor. Really it was from being exploited by the rubber bosses, who grew quite wealthy from the forest. Extractive reserves,

This poster shows Marina and Chico Mendes in their campaign for government office. Marina, for the first time, stepped into politics and public attention.

Marina speaks to a group of indigenous Kiaiowá people.

Marina explained, made sense in every way.

Opposition was powerful. Landowners and even settlers resented the idea of large areas set aside just for a few so-called backwards Indians and nut pickers. Landowners believed land was useful only for crops or cattle, and said so on TV and radio.

People in Acre were tired of poverty and isolation. They wanted the life they saw on television. Politicians promised them this to get votes. Marina knew people fantasized out of misery and desperation. But TV life would always be a fantasy without radical changes in Brazil's society. If people believed they had a voice in government and fully understood the issues, they would demand to live in their home—the forest—*with* schools, roads, and hospitals.

Marina worked tirelessly and spoke eloquently. Her educational efforts began to succeed; people understood the issues. But there was another big obstacle to winning elections: people wouldn't waste votes on someone who didn't have a chance.

Marina was the answer, the candidate who had a chance. She was very popular in her first campaign. Many more people voted for her than had ever voted for Chico, though he was better known, and she got more votes than most wealthy candidates. Her university degree made a huge difference.

It was around this time that Marina read Alice Walker's novel *The Color Purple,* about a poor African American woman in the American South. The connection she felt with the woman in the book was so intense she cried over the pages. Both of them had experienced a lifetime of suffering and inferiority. Marina was overwhelmed by the insight that such misery and oppression can hurt all that is best in each person and blot out the bright soul. But suddenly, with acceptance and love, this utterly unimportant person can feel pleasure and unlimited possibility.

Marina understood that every person needs to belong, every people needs identity. Nothing can replace the pain and delight of knowing oneself and being true to oneself. She chose ethics over tactics in public life—she wouldn't lie or cheat even to win an election.

Marina lost her fear of expressing emotions, and she affirmed the importance of love. Fábio Vaz de Lima, an agricultural expert from São Paulo was working to help the new rubber tapping cooperative in Xapuri. He shared Marina's deep love for the rainforest and belief in sustainable development. Here was someone with whom Marina could share her ideas, work, and commitment. Marina and Fábio married, and Fábio helped with Marina's next campaign.

In 1988, Marina ran for the Rio Branco city council. Acre's once-sleepy state capital was now a crowded city. Half the population of Acre lived there. Indigenous people, settlers, and *seringueiros* who had lost their homes overflowed Rio Branco's *favela*. From a few shacks along the river it grew to crowded communities of tens of thousands.

Once self-sufficient in the forest, now the *favelados* had nothing: no garden, no land to hunt and gather, no rainforest. Marina knew their hardships, and they knew she cared and worked for them.

Marina showed them their plight was not just hard luck, but linked to government policies. The government gave the ranchers handouts to come to Acre. The settlers lost their homes because of

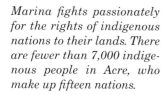

Marina fights passionately for the rights of indigenous nations to their lands. There are fewer than 7,000 indigenous people in Acre, who make up fifteen nations.

government mistakes. And the government gave away forest people's homes to ranchers. To change government policies *favelados* needed to become active citizens.

Marina and her friends organized rallies. Popular bands drew crowds to Marina's fiery speeches, which inspired Acreans to take a stand for justice and the forest. She spoke from experience of the daily struggle to survive, of the hurtful prejudice against the poor. She pointed out the connections between the ranchers' human rights abuses and corrupt government officials. Ranchers drove people from their homes at gunpoint, burned the forest, and beat and killed people who got in their way. Officials took bribes, abused their authority, and ignored ranchers' crimes and people's suffering.

People only had to look at the sky to see the results of the government's development projects. Despite the *empates,* more forest was burning than ever before. Smoke was so thick, airplanes couldn't land.

Why is biodiversity valuable?

Each living thing has a unique mix of genes and traits, called genetic diversity. Individual differences protect a species from extinction, or dying out, as the result of disease or climate change.

Biodiversity is the variety of life on the earth. There is not just one kind of butterfly, but many, and many kinds of trees, fish, and other organisms. Just as genetic diversity is the key to species survival, biodiversity is the key to our planet's survival—and to the rainforest's survival.

Amazonia contains at least one third of the earth's biodiversity. Medical researchers look to Amazonia for cures for diseases. Agricultural researchers look for ways to improve crops. Environmentalists preserve species for scientific and ethical reasons.

Brazil's government has promised to protect the rainforest by creating parks and reserves, but many of these are never made official. Laws protecting parks and reserves are not enforced, so illegal logging, mining, and burning of forests has grown worse than ever before. Scientists think that if this continues 20 percent of the world's species could be extinct in thirty years.

Everyone was coughing. The enormous smoke cloud erupting into the atmosphere shocked astronauts who saw it from the space shuttle.

Marina's efforts bore fruit. All classes of people found something to like or respect in her. A university degree brought enormous respect from ordinary people, and even the upper classes. In addition, she was a teacher and a mother, and had a reputation for caring about ordinary people.

She won the election. More people voted for her than any other candidate in any Acre campaign. She was the PT's first city councilor in Rio Branco.

Marina was outraged when she saw her first paycheck. Her salary was huge! Public money that could pay for clean water, schools, and health clinics was going into the pockets of officials who already had plenty. Marina couldn't accept this. She

This photo of smoke from burning forests in Amazonia was taken from the space shuttle as it orbited the earth. The vast smoke plumes swallowed up nearby storm clouds, some of which can be seen in the background.

showed her check to the Rio Branco television and newspapers. The large salaries and bonuses that politicians quietly accepted were made public for the first time.

Marina's unselfishness was a big surprise. It got the attention of small business people and the middle class, who respected and remembered her for it.

City officials were furious, especially when Marina filed a lawsuit forcing them to return some of the money they had collected in salaries. Marina wanted to clean up Acre. She wanted honesty, citizenship, and democracy. True democracy is impossible in secret, with huge gaps in power between rich and poor.

Despite Marina's hard work, she said God helped her succeed. "I always had the feeling I would never convince anybody just by my speeches," she said. "I had to be a dreamer thinking I could get this far." Her dream of a family grew, too, with a new daughter, Moara.

But that year did not end happily. In 1986, *empates*

made a giant meat company give up on ranching and sell its land. Other ranchers were furious and began terrorizing the *seringueiros*. Marina was shocked and grieved at the deaths of her friends. Her good friend Ivair Higino was shot in the back while he milked his family's cow. He had worked closely with Marina and Chico in the PT and Rural Workers Union.

Chico received many death threats. His family was afraid to leave the house, there were so many men with guns nearby threatening them. Marina knew Chico would die sooner or later, and he knew it, too. He went to the press, the police, to state officials, but they did almost nothing to help.

Marina was in São Paulo for health treatment the week before Christmas in 1988. Late one evening the telephone rang. It was Fábio's cousin, and his voice was sad. "Before he said anything I already knew Chico was dead," she remembered.

News of Chico's assassination flashed around the

At Chico Mendes's funeral, rubber tappers and union leaders who worked with Chico grieve his murder. Raimundo de Barros raises his fists and Julio Barbosa stands in front of him. Barbosa was later elected mayor of Xapuri.

globe. Brazil was embarrassed in the eyes of the world. Over a thousand activists had been assassinated in the past ten years; none of those murders were investigated.

Thousands of people came to his funeral in Xapuri, and to services held around the world. The mourners took a vow: "I promise before the blood of our companion Chico Mendes to continue this work, to show our enemies that they will never succeed in silencing the voice of the *seringueiros.*" In São Paulo, Marina took part in a mass held in Chico's memory. "They killed Chico," she said, "but not his ideas." Leaders like Chico and Marina made a tremendous difference in the *seringueiros'* lives. None of them would give up.

"It was a great loss to the rubber tappers and to the movement to preserve the Amazon. They couldn't have been more wrong in their thinking that if they killed Chico they would be killing the movement. What happened was quite the contrary. The movement got even bigger and stronger," Marina said. "As

Who was Chico Mendes?

Francisco Alves "Chico" Mendes Filho led the fight to save the Amazon rainforest. When Chico was eighteen, a revolutionary who was hiding from the government in the deep forest taught him how to read and write and about politics. Chico went on to found workers' unions, and helped found the National Council of Seringueiros and the Alliance of the Peoples of the Forest, important organizations working to protect forest peoples' rights and land.

Books were written about him and films about him were shown on television. Environmentalists flew him to the United States to testify before congress about rainforest destruction. As a result of his life and death, plans to destroy natural environments around the world for the sake of development have been stopped or changed.

Rubber tappers and activists from across Brazil joined the crowds at Chico Mendes's funeral in Xapuri, Acre, December 25, 1988, along with family, friends, the local community, and environmentalists from around the world. In other parts of Brazil, memorials were painted on walls and people grieved the loss of such an important leader.

for my part, I will continue to carry on in Chico's name for as long as I can."

Chico's murder *was* investigated. The ranchers who killed him were eventually arrested and imprisoned. The 2.5 million acre Cachoeira Seringal, where Chico was born, is now the Chico Mendes Extractive Reserve. It covers 6 percent of Acre, including every *seringal* Chico fought for.

Chapter 7

CARRYING THE DREAM TO THE GOVERNMENT

The end of the 1980s were exciting years in Brazilian politics. The military gave over power to a president chosen by congress. New political parties made up a new congress that began working on a new constitution. Voting laws were changed; now everyone could vote. In 1989, after mass demonstrations organized by the PT, the first presidential election in almost thirty years was held. Tens of millions of Brazilians who had never cast a vote for a president came close to electing Lula.

The PT had more support and more money to help its candidates than in the past. Marina took Acre by surprise with her thunderous televised speeches against government corruption. She spoke out about the injustice of Brazil's worst wound: the gap between rich and poor that created the environmental devastation around them. In 1990 Marina was elected representative to Acre's state congress.

Marina was incredibly popular with the poor of Acre. There was no one like her: a rubber tapper, born poor as they were, with a university degree. More miraculous was the fact that Marina had not forgotten them in her good fortune. She helped get them more schools and health clinics. She attacked governors' luxurious retirement benefits.

That year she worked with an environmental

At demonstrations across Brazil people came together to support laws to make reserves in the rainforest.

Are women represented in governments around the world?

There are few women in most governments. Women in most democratic countries were not allowed to vote until the middle of the twentieth century. Women now in national law-making assemblies are four out of ten in Norway, three out of ten in countries like Sweden and Finland, two out of ten in China and Canada, and in the United States are just about one out of every ten members of congress. In Brazil one in twenty senators are women. Over forty countries have no women lawmakers, and over a dozen have no women at all in powerful government jobs. Women chosen to be advisers to governments are mostly assigned to work with health, housing, education, and other areas traditionally thought of as women's issues. But women have important views on money, armed forces, relationships with other countries, and everything governments do.

On the other hand, the number of women in governments worldwide has more than doubled in the past fifteen years. Throughout history, many countries have had women presidents, prime ministers, or military leaders. In the past century women have led Argentina, Bolivia, Dominica, Haiti, Nicaragua, Great Britain, Ireland, India, Israel, Pakistan, the Philippines, and Turkey.

All kinds of people need to be represented in governments because there are many different views and needs among the people of every country. A woman who gathers nuts in Amazonia has different problems from a businessman in São Paulo, just as a Montana rancher worries about different issues than a working mother in New York.

organization on a campaign to change policies of the World Trade Organization. A powerful international organization, the WTO controls how countries run their business with other countries. But the WTO makes decisions based on what is good for trade, not what is good for the environment. Marina learned more about how rich countries affect life in Acre. Protection for Amazonia would mean changing how the whole world does business.

As a state official, she could act against foreign business in Acre that threatened the environment.

Many officials accept bribes to vote in business's favor, or to ignore illegal activities in the forest. Marina exposed corruption and worked to enforce environmental laws. Every debate in Acre's congress was a chance for her to teach and to learn about others' viewpoints. Her goal was to find solutions. She didn't want to just win arguments—she wanted others to see the rainforest in new ways.

After her first year in office, on a trip deep in the rainforest, Marina suddenly became extremely ill. She was rushed to the Rio Branco hospital. She had pain, weakness, and other problems doctors couldn't explain, and it got worse. With help from Lula and friends in the PT, she flew to São Paulo for better tests.

The experts were mystified. It was Marina herself who figured out the problem. "My mouth tasted strange, as if I had a coin in it, and I told everybody that I was contaminated by metals. But the tests would not detect it, and nobody believed me."

In a magazine she saw the name of a specialist. Samples of her hair were sent to the United States for analysis. She was right. Her liver, nervous system,

At a demonstration to gain rights for indigenous people, Marina stands up to a soldier blocking the path of the marchers, while reporters with television cameras watch. The support of people who learn about a protest from television or newspapers can sometimes help pressure a government to make changes.

When Marina got sick from chemical poisoning, she began using a cane until she could get treatment. But she continued her work, speaking and listening to activists and workers.

and some other organs were damaged by mercury. Mercury from gold mining contaminates many rivers in Amazonia, getting into fish and other foods.

Treatment to remove the mercury from her body could not begin because Marina was pregnant. The treatment was dangerous for her baby. Her daughter Mayara was born in mid-1992, and Marina began the treatment. Regaining her health was slow. For a year she could hardly work. Her strict diet avoided processed and canned food. Her passionate energy would suddenly run out in the midst of activity. She had to rest before going on.

Illness taught her to take care of herself as well as others. She had been so strong as a girl that the limits of her strength came as a surprise. "A strong soul is not enough to keep you alive," she says. "You need a healthy body, too."

Though it slowed her pace, Marina couldn't let

In the federal senate Marina was able to speak to national lawmakers about extractive reserves, and to convince a majority to vote for the law written by rubber tappers, environmentalists, and by Marina herself. She was one of the first people who was not from a wealthy family to serve in the senate.

poor health stop her. If she was suffering, *favelados,* indigenous people, and landless families suffered more. She kept writing new laws and speaking whenever she could, accomplishing more than any other state representative, despite her long illness.

In the 1994 elections PT candidates in Acre ran for governor, mayor of Rio Branco, and local councils. PT candidates ran in other states, too. Marina, the most popular candidate Acre had ever seen, ran for federal senator. Although she still felt sick, she began the long, hard campaign. She traveled all over Acre to talk with people. Marina went by car, boat, and plane, as well as by horse and on foot.

Her rich rivals included a former governor, a former senator, and a businessman who was from the party that controlled the newspaper and TV station. Marina won her opponents' respect with her honesty, intelligence, and determination. The businessman called her "a tornado." Despite polls that showed Marina would lose, she triumphed again. She defeated the wealthy candidates and received more votes than any senator in Brazil. She joined only four other women in Brazil's senate.

Marina's voter education efforts had succeeded. "Our campaign theme was an informed vote, and people understood our message." The people of Acre no longer passively followed a boss. A recent poll showed that 75 percent of the poor people in Acre wanted sustainable development. Marina pointed out that "ten years ago people wanted roads, ranches, progress—anything that looked like São Paulo or Rio de Janeiro—anything but the forest."

She called herself "the tip of an iceberg, in that I am the voice and fight of so many who are against the destruction of the Amazon, but who are in favor of developing it with sensitivity to its ecostructure and awareness of its impact on so many lives. This is why I became a senator."

She objected to the government's plans for agriculture in Amazonia. Usual crops and farming methods don't work in the rainforest; they destroy both forest and soil.

Marina supported new ways of farming that don't destroy the rainforest. Agroforestry mixes fast-growing crops with slower-growing coffee and trees. Such crops could be planted in cleared areas where ranchers have given up on the land.

Amazonia's biodiversity is too valuable to lose. Europe, much of the United States, and coastal Brazil were all once heavily forested. When the forest disappeared, so did biodiversity. "We are not going to suffer from the same devastation that occurred in Europe and the United States," Marina insisted.

Once she was in the senate, Marina Silva's mission

Cows graze in a pasture that was once rainforest. Diverse plants and animals, as well as varied resources that renew themselves, such as rubber, wood, fruit, and nuts, are often replaced by a one-product economy, such as cattle for beef.

was to change how Brazil—and the world—thought about Amazonia: not as a place to exploit, but as a resource to care for; not as empty space, but as home to millions of people and to the species of a priceless ecosystem.

As one of her first actions as senator, Marina wrote cutting-edge laws controlling Brazil's bioresources. Wealthy nations with little biodiversity of their own exploit the bioresources of tropical countries. Over 70 percent of drugs derived from plants came from Amazonia. Researchers believe cures for diseases like cancer, AIDS, and heart disease are hidden in tropical forests. To make new drugs and test for new cures, many scientists collected samples without permission. Dozens of plants used for indigenous medicine and religion were taken. The plants and their active ingredients were patented and sold, sometimes over the protests of indigenous peoples. Out of the millions of plants in the rainforest, indigenous people knew which plants were useful and showed them to

What happened to the idea of extractive reserves?

There are over twenty extractive reserves protecting more than 8 million acres of rainforest, all made law with the help of the National Council of Seringueiros. Groups of families form cooperatives and lease the reserves from the government. Cooperative members decide together how to use the land. Each time an issue is raised—for instance, whether to allow hunting with dogs or limited logging—every aspect is discussed until agreement is reached. This can take hours, days, or years. Amazonia's extractive reserves have become a model of sustainable development for communities around the world.

Millions of dollars have come from other countries to support the reserves. The government has built some health clinics and schools for the reserves, but doesn't help the extractivists with money, roads, and favors the way it does big farmers and ranchers.

researchers. Their sacred ceremonies are reduced to bottles of pills. Yet indigenous nations get none of the profits. Marina's laws would make this illegal.

"One fungus, one plant or insect could produce a product worth millions or billions of dollars," Marina pointed out. A portion of that money, returned to rainforest communities, would support sustainable development in Amazonia. Otherwise, forest communities have to make a living any way they can, which often means destructive logging or clearing forest for farming. "They know they have to stop because otherwise the wood will disappear," Marina said, but "there are no subsidies for natural rubber, they fear starvation." She fought for some government aid for Amazon rubber and won, but rubber tappers' lives remain poor and uncertain.

Some countries think bioresources belong to everyone. The United States and other wealthy nations have refused to sign the Convention on Biological Diversity, a treaty that 150 other countries have signed, that states that each country owns its own bioresources. One U.S. official said, "That anybody thinks they should get a share of the profits because they happen to be squatting on the forest where the resources are is laughable."

Marina's legislation was passed by the Federal Senate in 1998 but was stopped before it could be signed into law. The legislation would require researchers to fill out long applications and get permits to take samples, and give part of their profits to rainforest communities and indigenous nations.

Marina worked to solve the double problem of preserving the rainforest and developing Amazonia by fighting for more extractive reserves. She was the

Thousands of species of orchids, bromeliads, and other plants live on rainforest trees without any soil at all. They have evolved to live with particular species of insects, reptiles, frogs, or birds, and each would die out without the other.

leading sponsor of the Environmental Crimes Act, which meant deforestation and illegal logging would be punished for the first time. Ranchers opposed this law fiercely. If people couldn't get rich from the forest illegally, Marina hoped, extractive reserves would have a better chance.

Also, for extractive reserves to succeed, more people needed to be able to buy forest products. Marina worked with Brazilian officials on a solution. Several states used her plan to buy Brazil nuts for school lunches. Both nut gatherers and hungry children benefitted.

Other countries buy many useful forest products, too. "People who support sustainable development know that it is not a challenge for any single nation. It is a challenge for humanity and so must be shared among us." She met with U.S. President Bill Clinton in 1997 and discussed how the United States could help Amazonia with equipment and trade. She criticized American and European businesses that buy rubber from plantations in Asia, where workers are treated horribly.

While Brazil's senate was in session, Marina gave a speech every few days. She called attention to current events like mass suicides in indigenous nations, violence over farmland, and the discovery of enslaved workers in isolated areas. She reminded the senate of ongoing problems like health care, hunger, discrimination, and violence against children, the poor, women, and minorities. The rich senators can't just ignore someone who speaks for millions of people.

Marina worked with progressive senators like Benedita da Silva, who in 1982 became the first black woman to be elected to a city council in Brazil.

This harlequin frog is poisonous. Over millions of years, birds who live nearby have developed an instinct not to eat the bright yellow and black frog. Frogs help rainforest plants by eating insects and pollinating flowers. Each creature in an ecosystem is adapted to live together, as puzzle pieces fit together. The extinction of one member of an ecosystem can affect the survival of all the others.

A mountain of Brazil nuts, gathered from the forest by hand, piles up at a cooperative on an Amazonian extractive reserve. Each person at the reserve contributes their work and gets an equal share of the benefits. When people in other countries buy Brazil nuts, it helps extractive reserves and protects the rainforest.

They worked on the important issues of farmland, foreign debt, and poverty. They were both immune to the wealth around them. Benedita da Silva said, "My interest in politics is not for personal gain, but to act as a voice for the voiceless. My aim is to help gain access to power for groups that have traditionally been locked out."

Just as the poor have been locked out of democracy in Brazil, Brazil and many other nations are locked out of economic power in the world. Brazil's enormous foreign debt, one of the largest in the world, limits how much the government can help the *seringueiros.* So much of the government's money leaves the country that very little is left for the environment and poor Brazilians.

In 1998 there was a crisis. Brazil could not repay what it owed to rich countries. To keep up payments, the government borrowed more money through the International Monetary Fund. The IMF has strict rules, however. Brazil was forced to make huge cuts

A community in Amazonia works together to build houses, schools, and health clinics for families of the rubber tappers, nut collectors, and other extractivists.

in programs to help *seringueiros* and to protect the environment. The cuts stopped research to find new ways of using Amazon land and products. Rainforest that was cleared takes hundreds, maybe thousands of years to return to the way it was. But without research, no one knows how to help it happen faster.

Benedita da Silva commented, "I get so angry when I think of how we could use the 10 billion dollars we pay the Western banks every year. It would be enough to build tens of thousands of health clinics or millions of low-income homes. It would allow us to . . . make a real difference in the lives of millions of poor Brazilians."

Marina and many other Latin Americans felt the heavy burden of Brazil's debt was unfair. When the loans came into Brazil, a lot of the money went into corrupt politicians' private bank accounts. The poor and middle-class people who suffer to repay it never

Why is foreign debt a problem?

Poor countries borrow money from richer countries for big development projects. Wealthy nations and international banks like to lend money because they make a profit on the loan's interest, the extra amount charged every year until the debt is paid back. Most poor nations are in the global south: Africa, Asia, and Latin America. Most rich nations are in the global north: Europe and North America.

Owing so much money puts poor countries like Brazil under the control of powerful countries like the United States, so that they can't always say no to development projects. The United States may want Brazil to take money to build more roads, even though that would hurt the ecology. Businesses from the global north also are allowed to move in and exploit and hurt the environment, while local homes and jobs are lost.

Under this system, the whole world is like *aviamento*: the rich northern nations are getting richer while the poor southern nations get poorer.

Marina, church leaders, and rubber tappers meet with the Brazilian president to discuss illegal logging on the reserves. Helping people from local communities communicate with the highest levels of government has been one of Marina's important achievements.

got anything from the loans. In fact, their lives were made worse by highways, dams, and other misguided projects.

"We cannot fix the past," Marina said. "The developed countries did not have the understanding that we now have while they were developing. But today we have learned that their way is not the right way. So developed and developing countries have to be partners in creating a new path."

Just as Marina stood with Chico to block bulldozers from the forest, she stood in the senate to block a new wave of Amazonian development. In the capital, Brasília, among the artificial lakes, modern sculptures, and space age buildings, Marina used the law to fight for the forest and its peoples.

Chapter 8

"TO THE FUTURE, THAT'S WHERE I'LL GO"

Before Marina's arrival in the elegant, blue-carpeted senate hall, when the senate discussed dams, mines, or highways, the rights of the people affected by these projects were dismissed. The senate preferred to overlook the needs of *seringueiros,* indigenous people, and poor farmers. When there was disagreement, the senators said whatever helped them politically, rather than what was best for the country.

Now Marina is heard. She speaks passionately yet thoughtfully, and takes her job very seriously. She studies every bill before it's debated—as few senators do.

When she speaks of Amazonia, she speaks with authority. Even those who disagree with her know she doesn't guess or imagine things the way she'd like them to be; she has the facts, and knows the people and the issues.

Marina listens. She takes in each point of view, each group's concerns and needs. Then, with a style and vision all her own, she knits these different threads together into a workable plan. She doesn't sit back in her office; when she hears of a problem she goes there herself. She is fond of quoting Albert Einstein, saying, "If I am able to see a little farther than others, it is because I am supported by the shoulders of giants." For Marina these "giants" are

This moth has two sets of eye-shaped spots that reflect the sun and frighten predators. The rainforest is home to millions of species of insects, most still unknown to science.

ordinary people—*seringueiros*, indigenous people, and scientists.

Marina and other like-minded senators support each other's efforts to win social justice for forest people, *favelados,* women, blacks, and other minorities. As senators they can make laws that enforce Brazil's new constitution and help create true democracy.

Marina educates people about being consumers. Corporations constantly need more consumers to buy the things they make. They think up new things for people to want, and take more of the earth's resources to make things, and to make packages for things. But Marina insists that things don't make people happy. Only connection with real life—people, nature, and meaning—can do that. With all Brazil's things—sophisticated industry, advanced weapons and technology, mines, dams, highways—her country has not been able to lessen illiteracy or poverty, or give people better lives.

Thousands of species live in the countless rivers and streams of Amazonia, like the piranha, anaconda, river dolphin, and giant otter. People swim, bathe, and drink from the water, and also depend on fish for food. This kind of resource cannot be bought or sold.

"This is a great contradiction," Marina says. "And the core of this contradiction, it seems to me, is a model of consumption that is not based on satisfying or meeting the needs of *being,* but of meeting the needs of *having.* This is perverse. So we need to change this model." She warns, "If we continue along the path that we are going, we'll ultimately destroy ourselves."

Her opponents accuse Marina of standing in the way of progress. Actually, she welcomes progress that truly makes people's lives better. Progress is more and better food, meaningful and satisfying work, better education and health care, cleaner air and water. Marina is one of Brazil's few environmentalists who believe that logging and roads, planned carefully, can help Amazonia.

Like everyone else, Marina sometimes feels sad or discouraged. So many heros, friends, children, and loved ones have died, and the assassinations and suffering continue every day. The power of her vision can't always overcome the misery around her, especially when she feels tired and her health is poor—the continuing effect of the damage her body suffered from mercury poisoning.

But her people lift her up again. Their faces light with pride when they see her, and their eyes fill with hope. She is one of them, *their* senator, living proof of the dream they share.

Like all forest people, Marina has a deep connection to the forest. She sees nature as an equal partner in human life. To her, the health of the body and the health of the soul are not separate. True love for humanity must be accompanied by a reverence for nature.

How can you help save the rainforest?

The best hope for the rainforest lies in the world paying attention to its plight. Each person can help in small ways. Eating Brazil nuts and other rainforest foods helps. Ask for furniture made of wood that was logged sustainably, and natural Amazonian rubber in mattresses. By asking for products that help the rainforest instead of hurting it, you let businesses know that you think about what you buy.

Your government can do a lot to help extractive reserves. Tell your senators and representatives that you care about the rainforest and extractive reserves. Ask them what they are doing to help. Web sites and other resources (like those at the back of this book) provide strategies for helping the rainforest and rainforest communities.

When protestors in Seattle in 1999, and Washington, D.C., in 2000, demonstrated against the International Monetary Fund, the World Trade Organization, and the World Bank, Brazilians were very happy. They see this as solidarity of ordinary people in the United States with Brazil's struggles.

Marina speaks firmly and passionately for a new vision of society. Brazil's mixed peoples, cultures and ancestors are the nation's true identity, not the terrible split between rich and poor. She writes, "The human race is complete when everyone is living free and appreciating our natural difference. The quality of love is the greatest gift we have for the future. To go forward, we must begin right there: end all racial prejudice, everything, all kinds of separation."

In Brazil the gap between rich and poor is one of the largest in the world, with 5 percent of the population owning 95 percent of the farmland, and 70 percent of the population considered poor. Rich and poor live completely separated, as if in different worlds. This separation echoes the other great separation Marina sees in the world, that between humanity and nature. "The great human challenge

Vines thicker than arms, like this one, weave through the trees and make paths in the air for monkeys, jaguars, and crawling animals. All life in the rainforest is interconnected. Tropical rainforests are the oldest ecologies on earth, sixty million years of complex connections between species.

is to balance these two," she writes. "They are sick because they are separated."

She works to heal this sickness. "Our great challenge is to force the government to just finance projects that comply with environmental and social impact studies and promote sustainability." Marina has tried to include this requirement on the federal budget legislation, calling it the Social Budget. It has been rejected so far. She will keep trying. In the state of Acre, she has worked with Governer Jorge Viana on a similar budget project.

"When I really dream I think we should come up with solutions to show the world. What country besides Brazil could have this?" With its vast rainforest, traditional peoples, and high technology Brazil could become a world leader by showing a new vision of society working with nature.

Solidarity among the people of Brazil and the nations of the world is an important piece of her vision. In her life, when she was in need, people helped her with medicine, election campaigns, and knowledge. People didn't expect favors in return. They helped out of solidarity, belief in their mutual goals.

"When I see that someone is discouraged by my side, I feel challenged to help them recover their passion, utopia, and dreams." When people dream together, the dream becomes reality.

Just as Marina healed the forest as a child, she fights now to heal Brazil. Many believe the only way to heal the wound between rich and poor is to redistribute farmland. "I defend private property," Lula says, "but for everybody. We cannot allow one man to own 25 million acres when others are starving."

Brazil's constitution allows the government to

take—with payment—unused farmland to give to landless farmers. But landowners are well represented in congress, so the law is not put into action. Instead the government sends landless farmers to settle Amazonia, where their farms fail and their children die of malaria.

There is a food shortage in Brazil. Over 80 percent of Brazil's food is grown on small farms, on less than 12 percent of the farmland. Yet big businesses continue to grow food for sale outside Brazil.

The small farmers organized and found another way. Dozens of families camp out and begin to farm idle land. If they stay long enough, the government must give them the land. Although the families are often met with violence, their efforts have brought national attention to their plight.

Education is still very important to Marina. She serves on the Senate Education Committee, and wrote a book on the subject. When she says, "Education

A rubber tapper stands at the base of a rainforest tree. The land around the tree was cleared. It will take decades for trees to grow back, and centuries for the full ecology to recover, if ever.

is the base of everything," her personal experience adds weight to her words. But, she says, "It is an effort for everyone. It is true that in other parts of Brazil education is bad, but in the Amazon region, it is twice or three times as bad." The illiteracy rate in Amazonia is still over 40 percent. "Education is essential since it creates new cultural values: avoiding prejudice and persecution," she says.

Marina hopes new cultural values will lead to equality, instead of rich, powerful men at the top. "Thousands of people die while we are producing weapons. Thousands of people die because of hunger while the financial system accumulates money." She envisions the unjust ideas behind the system breaking down. People will discuss their views with respect and tolerance for one another's differences.

She sees leaders unite their countries and cultures, but too often turn their backs to their people's needs. Her own model of a leader is to be led, both by the people and by her conscience. She respects Nelson Mandela of South Africa as a leader who speaks only after listening, and who lets the people show him how to help them.

She says, "This thing about power is kind of funny to me. I don't feel like I have power." Yet her name appeared recently in Brazil's most popular weekly news magazine, *Veja,* on a list of the six most influential politicians.

Marina's intelligent and passionate leadership has been recognized outside of Brazil. In 1996, she was awarded the respected Goldman Environmental Prize. Each year, a grassroots environmental activist is chosen from each continent to receive the $100,000 cash prize.

Marina holds her Goldman environmental award, which she received in 1996 to recognize her leadership of empates *and her work to stop deforestation.*

In 1997, Marina was among twenty-five of the world's women chosen by the United Nations Environmental Program to receive an award in honor of International Women's Day and UNEP's twenty-fifth anniversary. Also in 1997, she was one of *Ms.* magazine's Women of the Year.

Though she still describes herself as shy and driven by faith, Marina was the first to break an unwritten rule of women's fashion and wear long pants into the senate. "Born and raised in the forest, I never imagined I'd be dressed in ladies suits and high heels." She has her own style that ignores fashion trends. "I don't like the pomp and ritual aspects of the senators' routine," she admits.

Relaxing means seeing a movie or curling up with the Bible, a book on psychology or spirituality, or a favorite novel. She makes a point of daily exercise,

Marina is at her office in Acre with her children, Danilo, Moara, Mayara, and Shalon, and Sonia, the daughter of a coworker.

Bible study, and prayer. Marina says that, like Mahatma Gandhi, she sees her life as an example to others, so she lives in the best way she knows.

Time with her husband and children is precious. The closeness and connection she feels with them, their warmth and caring, carry her through the hard work in the senate and her struggles with poor health. She remains close with her other family members. Her father stays with her often in Brasilia. Three of Marina's sisters still live on their land in the former Seringal Bagaço. They never treated Marina any differently because she went to college and became a senator. In her family, everyone is admired for their own special qualities.

"We must affirm our point of view," she says to young women. "Don't give up your dreams." In spite of all her life's challenges, she has never given up her essential dreams, "not even for my kids, or my father, or for a man that I love. Exactly because of that my father, my kids, and this man love me."

Marina is loved and admired not only by her family, but by millions of people in Brazil and the world. To them, she represents personal strength, community solidarity, respect for the natural environment, and hope for the future. Marina's slogan is, "To the future, that's where I'll go," bringing her people with her.

CHRONOLOGY

1958	Maria Osmarina da Silva is born on February 8 in Seringal Bagaço, in the state of Acre.
1964	A military regime replaces Brazil's democratically elected government.
1966	Marina's family moves to Manaus, then to Santa Maria, Pará, hoping for a better life.
1969	The family moves back to Acre, penniless and hungry.
1970	The family pays off its debt to the rubber boss. The highway and settlers reach Rôndonia and Acre, bringing disease and clearing land.
1973	Seringal Bagaço is broken up into plots for farming. Marina's family gets ownership of their land.
1974	Marina's older sister is married. Her mother and two younger sisters die of epidemic illnesses.
1975	Marina is ill with hepatitis. At age sixteen, she moves to Rio Branco for medical treatment and begins school.
1976	The first *empate* is held to block clearing of rainforest land. Marina enters the convent to study and to become a nun. Chico Mendes founds the Xapuri chapter of the Rural Workers Union.
1977	Marina meets Chico Mendes.
1978	Marina finishes high school.
1980	Marina marries Raimundo Gomes de Souza. She passes the university entrance exams. Wilson Pinheiro is assassinated by ranchers. The PT, or Workers' Party, comes to Acre.
1981	Marina's first daughter, Shalon, is born.

1982	The regime legalizes other political parties. The first open elections are held, and PT candidates run. Marina's son, Danilo, is born.
1984	Marina and Chico co-found the Xapuri chapter of CUT, the Central Workers Union. Marina graduates from the university.
1985	Maria ends her marriage to Raimundo.
1986	Marina marries Fábio Vaz de Lima. Brazil elects representatives to write a new constitution.
1988	Running with the PT, Marina is elected to the Rio Branco city council. Her second daughter, Moara, is born. Chico Mendes is assassinated by ranchers. Later, the first extractive reserve is created and named for him.
1990	Marina is elected Acre state representative.
1991	Marina becomes ill with mercury poisoning.
1992	Marina's third daughter, Mayara, is born, and Marina begins treatment to remove the mercury from her body.
1994	Marina is elected to the federal senate, taking on the struggle to protect the environment and promote sustainable development.
1995	Marina proposes legislation to regulate bioresources and traditional knowledge.
1996	Marina is awarded the Goldman Environmental Prize.
1997	Marina is a *Ms.* magazine Woman of the Year. Marina is one of twenty-five women honored by the United Nations Environment Program.
1998	Marina's biodiversity legislation is approved by the Federal Senate.
1999	Marina assumes senate leadership of the PT and opposition. She proposes the Social Budget and a commission to combat poverty.

GLOSSARY

agroforestry A method of tropical forest farming that mixes crops of different heights and harvest times.

anthropologist Someone who studies human cultures.

aviamento The system that keeps poor rubber tappers in constant debt to landowners.

biodiversity The variety of different kinds of organisms in a region or on the earth.

bioresources Living resources such as plants and genetic information from people.

class A group of people within a society who share a similar economic situation, education, and often many aspects of daily life. Elite, upper class, middle class, working class, and poor are examples of class distinctions.

constitution The legal document that describes the laws, principles, and organization of a government, and the rights of a nation's people.

democracy A political system in which a nation's people vote to elect officials to represent them at all levels of government.

development Replacing natural environments with human ones to make money and improve people's lives.

ecology The way in which every species of plant, animal, and organism in an area works together.

ecosystem All of the species that evolved to live in balance together in a particular area.

elite Wealthy, powerful people in society who inherited their wealth and power, and who often consider themselves the very best.

empate [em-POTCH-ay] Action by rubber tappers to halt rainforest destruction.

exploit To take for one's own use or profit without a fair return.

extractive reserves Rainforest areas set aside for use only by communities of people who extract their living from the forest sustainably.

favela A slum in a Brazilian city.

favelado Someone living in a *favela*.

federal A political system in which states are ruled in certain ways by a central government.

gender roles Aspects of life assigned to women or girls, men or boys, because of their sex. Jobs, behaviors, clothing, language, careers, and interests can all be affected.

indigenous people The original people living in an area before foreign invasion or colonization.

Latin America The countries of the Caribbean, Central America, and South America, which were colonized originally by Spain, France, or Portugal.

nordestino Someone from Brazil's northeast region.

seringal [say-reeng-GAHL] A region of rainforest in which rubber trees are tapped for latex.

seringueiro [SAY-reeng-GAY-row] A rubber tapper.

subsidy When a government gives money to encourage people or companies that produce certain goods or crops.

sustainable development Increasing the income and standard of living of a region without harming the environment or using up resources.

union An organization that unites workers to speak with one voice in negotiations with their employers.

FURTHER READING

Books about Amazonia and the environment

DeStefano, Susan. *Chico Mendes: Fight for the Forest.* Earthkeepers. Frederick, MD: Twenty-First Century Books, 1992.

Gallant, Roy A. *Earth's Vanishing Forests.* New York: Atheneum, 1992.

Krensky, Stephen. *Four Against the Odds: the Struggle to Save Our Environment.* New York: Scholastic, 1992.

Lewington, Anna. *Antonio's Rain Forest.* Minneapolis: Carolrhoda, 1993.

Schwartz, David M. *Yanomami: People of the Amazon.* New York: Lothrop, Lee & Shepard Books, 1995.

Silverstone, Michael. *Winona LaDuke: Restoring Land and Culture in Native America.* New York: The Feminist Press, 2001.

Tangley, Laura. *The Rainforest.* Earth at Risk. Broomall, PA: Chelsea House Publishers, 1992.

Internet Sites

Acre Amazon Link: www.amazonlink.org

Amanaka'a Amazon Network: www.amanakaa.org

Environmental Defense Fund's Chico Mendes Sustainable Rainforests Campaign:www.edf.org/programs/International/chico

Global Exchange: www.globalexchange.org

National Wildlife Federation: www.nwf.org

Rainforest Alliance: www.rainforest-alliance.org

World Wildlife Fund: www.worldwildlife.org

Films/Videos

The Burning Season: The Chico Mendes Story. Directed by John Frankenheimer, produced by John Frankenheimer, Thomas M. Hammel, and David Puttman, 1994. Distributed by Home Box Office, Warner Home Video.

The Decade of Destruction. Written and directed by Adrian Cowell, produced by Roger James, 1990. Distributed by Bullfrog Films.

Ceremony Presentation Tape, 1996 Goldman Environmental Prize. Produced by the Goldman Environmental Foundation, 1997.

Green Fire: Lives of Commitment and Passion in a Fragile World. Written and directed by Sue Cohn, 1999. United Nations Environmental Programme (UNEP).

INDEX

Page numbers in *italic* type indicate photo captions

Dedication

This book is dedicated to Marina Silva and to the memory of all those who gave their lives in the struggle against deforestation in the Amazon.

Acknowledgments

My deepest thanks to Marina Silva for her assistance and her inspiring example. I am especially grateful to Nilo Diniz and others at Senator Silva's office who helped, and to Steve Schwartzman for his indispensable aid, generosity, and wealth of knowledge. My heartfelt gratitude goes also to Anna Stuart, Beto Borges, Stephen R. King, Steve Kurtz, and Merrilee Mardon for their generous sharing of their expertise, without which I could not have written this book. Special thanks also to Christine Halvorson, Solange Lira, Sue Cohn, Julene Freitas, Madeleine Cousineau, Joanne Fox-Przeworski, Valdir Cruz, and Fr. Leo Hoar. Thanks to Denise MacLennan and Luly Fischer, Sally Siddiqi, Daphne Patai, Michael Schmidlehner, Betsy Ross, and the many friends and acquaintances who helped. Blessings on the Valley librarians, especially Judith, and the ILL folks at WMRLS. Thanks to my editor, Amanda Hamlin, and The Feminist Press. I am grateful to all who read the manuscript. My deep appreciation to my mother, husband, and daughter, and a bow with flourish to Michael Silverstone.

Picture Credits

Courtesy of José Caldas/SocialPhotos: 14, 32; Adrian Cowell/ Hutchison Library: 20, 29, 39, 45, 79, 81, 99; José Cruz/Social Photos: 84; Nilo Diniz: 62; Ricardo Funari/SocialPhotos: 21, 24, 34, 35, 37, 42, 44, 49, 60, 84, 91, 92; Goldman Environmental Foundation/Paul LaToures: 100; NASA/ Goddard Space Flight Center: 52, 54, 78; Edward Parker: 43; Photo-disc: 30; J. R. Ripper/SocialPhotos: 27, 31, 56, 61, 63, 65, 82; Alexandre Sant'Anna: 12; Stephan Schwartzman: 71; Nancy Sefton: 15, 16, 17, 26, 28, 38, 87, 89, 90, 94, 95, 98; Marina Silva/the office of Senator Marina Silva: 51, 58, 69, 73, 74, 76, 86, 93, 101; Nigel Smith/Hutchison Library: 47; Ricardo Stuckert: 57; Mário Variola: 85.

About the Author

Ziporah Hildebrandt is a writer, counselor, gardener, and homeschool parent. A graduate of Hampshire College, she has taught writing there and in her community. She is the author of numerous articles, essays, poems, stories, and books. She lives in western Massachusetts with her husband and daughter. Her website is www.ravensridgebookworks.com.